SpringerBriefs in Law

SpringerBriefs present concise summaries of cutting-edge research and practical applications across a wide spectrum of fields. Featuring compact volumes of 50 to 125 pages, the series covers a range of content from professional to academic. Typical topics might include:

A timely report of state-of-the art analytical techniques

A bridge between new research results, as published in journal articles, and a contextual literature review

A snapshot of a hot or emerging topic

A presentation of core concepts that students must understand in order to make independent contributions

SpringerBriefs in Law showcase emerging theory, empirical research, and practical application in Law from a global author community. SpringerBriefs are characterized by fast, global electronic dissemination, standard publishing contracts, standardized manuscript preparation and formatting guidelines, and expedited production schedules.

Rakiya Farah

Rereading Identity Deception in the UK Sexual Offences Act 2003

Incorporating Personal Traits and Attributes

Springer

Rakiya Farah
Magdalen College
Oxford, UK

ISSN 2192-855X ISSN 2192-8568 (electronic)
SpringerBriefs in Law
ISBN 978-3-031-44474-6 ISBN 978-3-031-44475-3 (eBook)
https://doi.org/10.1007/978-3-031-44475-3

This Springer imprint is published by the registered company Springer Nature Switzerland AG
The registered company address is: Gewerbestrasse 11, 6330 Cham, Switzerland

Acknowledgements

I wish to thank Professor Jonathan Herring for his supervision of my original thesis, which became this book. I have benefited hugely from his expertise and ongoing support. I am also very grateful for his review of this draft as I worked to develop it.

Contents

Chapter 1
Introduction

1.1 Why Identity?

Personal identity debates tend to address the question of change and persistence over time. The personal identity 'problem' is a metaphysical puzzle with which theorists continue to grapple.[1] It arises as a philosophical question when considering the interests and obligations of individuals. It asks what is at the heart of personal identity—of unity across time. Are you the same person after suffering severe brain injury, or are you a different person? This question is of fundamental importance to our self-understanding as human and social beings.[2] Inseparable from ethical questions,[3] the concept is deeply embedded in our major institutions, and many of our social practices and institutions depend on it.[4] Indeed, it has been described as underpinning all rights and obligations.[5] However, the question of what it consists in, as well as its significance, is highly contested and richly debated.

To be more precise, there is no single personal identity problem or question. Rather, there are multiple questions, which vary in their nature and significance according to context. As Schechtman notes, this means that there is no single answer; rather, there are different answers, each responding to the nature of the question.[6] In the criminal law context, the relevance of personal identity is grounded

[1] For discussion, Perry (1972).

[2] Schechtman (2018).

[3] Foster and Herring (2017), p. 44.

[4] Gligorov and Vitrano (2011), p. 154.

[5] Reid (1865).

[6] Schechtman (2018), p. 1.

R. Farah, *Rereading Identity Deception in the UK Sexual Offences Act 2003*, SpringerBriefs in Law, https://doi.org/10.1007/978-3-031-44475-3_1

in its relationship to personhood and moral status.[7] Most obviously, it governs when someone can be the victim or perpetrator of a crime. The concept of legal responsibility requires a minimally autonomous agent,[8] with the requisite capacities to be held liable for wrongdoing.[9] The concept has clear relevance for interpersonal moral relations.[10] Yet, it is relatively underexplored within criminal law. In her account of the criminal legal person, Naffine observes the construction of an abstract legal subject who is (silently) male.[11] For Norrie, the abstract juridical individual of legal doctrine is a 'homuncular form', generating tensions and contradictions within criminal law. Such contributions support this book's rationale: that there are certain assumptions underpinning the approach to personal identity in the criminal law, and that these should be excavated and addressed.

Accordingly, I argue that personal identity arises as a normative question in the law's treatment of deceptive sex. The Sexual Offences Act 2003 (hereafter, 'the SOA' or 'the 2003 Act') takes an unduly restrictive view of identity. While prohibiting impersonation of other persons to obtain consent to sex,[12] it fails to account for its qualitative aspects. It assumes that the concept of identity is fixed. More plausibly, it is fluid, mutable and indeterminate. Whereas the impersonation provision depicts a trait less, atomistic subject, the law should reflect this complexity instead of obscuring it.

Take the following hypothetical example. Imagine that a person, Dave, pretends to be the famous sports personality David Beckham to secure Vanessa's consent to sex. David Beckham happens to be Vanessa's hero. She throws all caution to the wind and has sex with Dave, believing that he is David Beckham. Let us call this *Scenario A*. Now imagine a slightly different scenario. Again, Dave pretends to be David Beckham. But in this scenario, Vanessa knows David Beckham. She does not know him very well, but enough to satisfy the impersonation provision's 'known personally' requirement.[13] Perhaps Dave and David Beckham resemble each other, or Vanessa might be slightly intoxicated. In any case, Vanessa is taken in by Dave's deception. Let us call this *Scenario B*. These scenarios share common features: Dave has pretended to be someone he is not, he has done so intending to trick Vanessa into consenting to sex, and Vanessa has consented to sex to which she would not otherwise have agreed.[14] Despite these commonalities, it is only in *Scenario B* that Vanessa finds protection in law. Yet, the structure of the wrong is clearly the same. This does not seem right.[15]

[7] Foster and Herring (2017), p. 3.

[8] Tadros (2008), p. 91.

[9] Moore (2013), p. 183.

[10] Shoemaker (2021).

[11] Naffine (2019). See also Norrie (2014).

[12] S 76(2)(b).

[13] This requirement is discussed in Part III, Chap. 7.

[14] Whether the deception must cause V to consent is unclear, but it plausibly should.

[15] More is said about this in Chap. 4.

1.2 Equivalence Thesis

The main contribution of this book is an extended argument in the form of an equivalence thesis presented in three stages.[16] It aims to show that section 76(2)(b) (the impersonation provision) of the SOA should be read to include qualitative identity deception. The starting point is the current position in law that impersonation of an identifiable other person is prima facie impermissible.[17] This is numerical identity deception, at times referred to as 'two-body' impersonation for ease of exposition. *Equivalence Thesis A* (Earlier Self Impersonation) shows that this type of deception is equivalent to impersonation of one's own earlier self, also referred to as 'single body' impersonation. This claim is supported by means of a thought experiment, which draws upon the psychological criterion of reductionist personal identity theory.[18] *Equivalence Thesis B* (Fictitious Other Impersonation) engages critically with the case of *R v Devonald*[19] to argue that impersonating an earlier version of oneself is equivalent to impersonation of fictitious other persons. *Equivalence Thesis C* (Fictitious Self Impersonation) then shows that this is analogous to someone pretending to be a different *kind* of person himself. This amounts to qualitative identity deception. It follows that this is, equally, impermissible. To sum up, the claim of equivalence tracks from *Earlier Self Impersonation* to *Fictitious Other Impersonation*, to *Fictitious Self Impersonation*. The final stage of this argument appeals to the idea of the social, relational self[20] to account for the *degree* of change required in such deception. By means of a novel theoretical framework, different types of change are explored. This aims to support a richer understanding of the wrong of identity deception in sexual offences.

More formally, the argument is as follows.

Equivalence Thesis (A): Earlier Self Impersonation

$\mathbf{P^1}$: It is impermissible to engage in two-body numerical impersonation

$\mathbf{P^2}$: Single-body numerical impersonation and two-body numerical impersonation are, other things equal, on a par in terms of permissibility (equivalence)

$\mathbf{C^1}$: Therefore, single-body numerical impersonation is impermissible

[16] This argumentative structure is inspired by Otsuka's (1994) moral equivalence thesis.

[17] Sexual Offences Act 2003, s 76(2)(b).

[18] Parfit (1984); Locke and Nidditch (1979).

[19] [2008] EWCA Crim 527.

[20] Taylor (1992).

Equivalence Thesis (B): Fictitious Other Impersonation
P^1: It is impermissible to impersonate one's earlier self (per C^1)
P^2: Impersonating a fictitious other person and impersonating one's earlier self are, other things equal, on a par in terms of permissibility (equivalence)
C^2: Therefore, impersonating a fictitious other person is impermissible

Equivalence Thesis (C): Fictitious Self Impersonation
P^1: It is impermissible to impersonate a fictitious other person (per C^2)
P^2: Pretending to be a different *kind* of person oneself and fictitious other impersonation is, other things equal, on a par in terms of permissibility (equivalence)[21]
C^3: Therefore, pretending to be a different kind of person is impermissible

1.3 Methodological Approach

The literature is divided on the question of whether the metaphysical and the normative-practical aspects of identity theory should be treated separately. This reflects a more fundamental disagreement about the priority relation between identity and ethics.[22] Reasons to address both aspects together, moving beyond abstract, introspective theorising, are various. They include the view that the value of a theory partly depends on the appeal of its implications; ensuring that we understand the self fully;[23] the need to understand the self in non-ideal terms;[24] and accounting for the relevance of agency and ethical action for the self.[25] Thus, Wallace combines these lenses on the basis that the self is constituted—albeit differently—by each. As she argues, 'A theory of the self should not be so spare metaphysically that it doesn't give much of a conceptual framework for understanding in practice what selves really are.'[26] The opposite view, which treats the metaphysical and the practical separately, is motivated by a concern to ensure clarity,[27] to reflect the distinct nature of the questions,[28] and to ensure the appropriate division of labour in answering each

[21] This premise is argued for by means of a Substantial Difference Argument.
[22] Shoemaker (2021).
[23] Schechtman (2014, 2018); Korsgaard (2003).
[24] Christman (2004).
[25] Gallagher and Marcel (1999).
[26] Wallace (2019).
[27] Olson (1997).
[28] Velleman (2002).

question.[29] In this ('descriptive metaphysics')[30] approach, one is guided by "common sense" categories and orthodox philosophical approaches to personal identity.[31]

Those who think that the starting point should be the ethical question recognise the importance of practical and value concerns to our understanding of personal identity.[32] More radically, Eklund endorses a moral relevance assumption,[33] which treats the moral question as the only question of philosophical significance. On this view, the metaphysical claim is fully determined by normative theory. Thus, one could simply posit a socio-legal order using those criteria for the personal identity concept deemed morally appealing. Such a society may stipulate that A at time t2 is the same person as B at time t1 if and only if B at time t2 has the same set of selected *traits and attributes* that A had at time t1.[34] It seems that this way of structuring its concerns would not be prima facie objectionable. Furthermore, the finding in R v *Melin*[35] that status attributes could be identity-determining in certain circumstances is not worlds apart from stipulating, as above, that we should structure our concerns directly around such attributes when asking who or what a person is.

The conceptual question is closely related to that of methodology. It asks whether which criteria should guide our use of concepts, such as person. That is, should what a concept means depend on what we want it to describe? This calls into question the descriptive content of such concepts. Some argue that our use of a concept should be governed by the exigencies of a particular context or purpose (a 'deflationary position'),[36] or that certain concepts should be shaped by normative concerns about social justice.[37] Thus, for Dennett, the concept 'person' has two different meanings, one metaphysical and one moral.[38] This view underpins normative conceptual work, or 'conceptual ethics.'[39] For some, metaphysical theorising is a 'project of conceptual engineering.'[40] Thus, we might decide that the label person applies to an entity because being a person has certain legal implications that we think ought to apply to that entity. This corresponds to functionalism. Thus, the question is not whether it is intelligible to understand identity change in terms of a change in values, beliefs and commitments, but whether it is useful to do so.[41] On the opposite view, whether, from a moral and legal perspective, an entity is a person is a

[29] Olson (1997).

[30] Strawson (2004).

[31] Wallace (2019).

[32] Gallagher and Marcel (1999); Dennett (1976).

[33] Eklund (2004), pp. 503–505.

[34] I borrow this expository structure from Eklund (2015).

[35] [2019] EWCA Crim 557, [2019] QB 1063.

[36] Thomasson (2016).

[37] Haslanger (2012).

[38] Dennett in Rorty (1976), p. 176.

[39] See Plunkett (2015).

[40] Thomasson (2016).

[41] Moore (1985), p. 29, drawing on Stone's distinction between intelligibility and usefulness.

factual question.[42] For Moore, these concepts have, among other functions, a descriptive and explanatory function. Therefore, we should address the question of meaning as a factual matter. As he explains, '... the meaning of legal, ordinary, and moral concepts cannot be found solely in the consequences of authoritative utterance.'[43] The question is: Is this a correct use of the term?

Theorists also seek to transcend the limitations of prevailing philosophical accounts of personal identity. There is a large and diverse body of literature exploring new theories and refining old ones. The dominant rationale is that existing neo-Lockean accounts lack sufficient interpretative value, descriptive or normative.[44]

This book steers a middle-way, combining metaphysical discussion with normative argument. I use this approach to foreground deeper questions about the scope of consent-vitiating identity deceptions in law, while avoiding conflation of distinctive and independently significant issues. At the same time, I think moral and practical issues have a role to play in a philosophical account of personal identity. I adopt West's view that there may be no single answer to the personal identity problem.[45] Moreover, in the absence of a 'canonical conception' of identity,[46] I endorse pluralism. Thus, as Tobia suggests, we might endorse one criterion of personal identity for some purposes, and a different criterion for others.[47] The view I take in this book is that once we have an adequate grasp of the metaphysical space, we are justified in exploring normative-practical solutions. I, therefore, engage with multiple lenses—the abstract, metaphysical lens and the social-relational lens, alongside normative aspects that help to justify the arguments being made. I begin with the metaphysical aspect to anchor the subsequent discussion addressing moral and legal questions.

Finally, it is not intended for this book's abstract metaphysical reflections to be taken literally, especially given the complexity of this area. There is warranted scepticism about the place of metaphysics in law.[48] While noting the metaphysical basis of the criminal law, Moore cautions that the use of arguments that are 'ethereal, abstract, and without content' risks arbitrariness.[49] Hence, the approach of this book is not to assert fanciful or implausible metaphysical claims. Insights from the personal identity problem are employed primarily as a fulcrum to test our intuitions about impersonation and to critique the law's approach. It engages deeply with social and philosophical theory. This provides the basis of a theoretical framework to rethink identity, including how and why it matters in sexual offences. Moreover,

[42] Ibid, 29.

[43] Ibid, 30.

[44] Wallace (2019).

[45] West (2009), p. 90.

[46] Sider (2001).

[47] Tobia (2022).

[48] Moore (1985), p. 25.

[49] Ibid, 80.

the book respects the boundaries of the reidentification and characterisation questions,[50] crossing them only via a sound equivalence thesis that is grounded in positive law, and which reflects their independent significance. Overall, it is hoped that the book's conclusions could be accepted by legal theorists and practitioners with divergent views on personal identity.

1.4 Structure

This book develops an extended argument in the form of an equivalence thesis, which draws upon a neo-Lockean psychological account of personal identity. My aim is to establish the moral equivalence of qualitative identity deception alongside numerical. I do so by drawing on a richer model of the self to articulate the significance of qualitative identity in sexual offences. While noting that there is more than one potential route into this problem, I engage with *the reidentification question* to test the limits of the current law. It is likely that we could reach the same conclusion by entering the debate via *the characterisation question*.[51] But my approach has the advantage of being grounded in positive law. Because and insofar as the impersonation provision treats numerical identity as salient and worthy of legal protection, qualitative identity should also be brought within the scope of the SOA.

The book is divided into three parts and nine chapters. The first chapter introduces the subject of the book and includes background, structure, definitions, and methodological approach. **Part I** introduces the central question and situates it within the wider theoretical literature on identity. It draws on social theory to analyse the relation between law and identity. **Part II** engages with personal identity theories to determine the conception that will guide the book's thesis. It presents the case law on the impersonation provision, noting the way in which the common law has both developed and stalled. Finally, it presents a socio-relational framework for understanding identity in this context. **Part III** presents the equivalence thesis. Concluding remarks are provided in the final chapter. Given the complex and extended nature of the argument, I shall outline this structure in more detail. The important point to note is the unifying argumentative thread which extends across the chapters, each part building on the preceding part/s.

Chapter 2 reviews the literature on identity, analysing law's problem with identity and grounding the relevant concepts of identity in social theory. The aim is not only to ensure that this work is theoretically grounded, but also to reap the benefits of bringing the social sciences and social theory into dialogue. Chapter 3 examines the concept of the person in sexual offences law, highlighting the relation between law

[50] Schechtman (2018).

[51] For more on this distinction, see Schechtman (2018).

and sexual autonomy. Chapter 4 argues that qualitative identity deception shares the same underlying rationale as that which animates the impersonation provision.

Chapter 5 prepares the ground for the main argument to follow. It explores theories of personal identity, while noting different approaches—metaphysical, practical, and moral. This chapter settles on the psychological criterion as an Archimedean point, considering that this is the most cited account and is, at least, a necessary condition of identity persistence. It presents developments in the empirical literature, which should lead us to question the dichotomy between identity and similarity. Chapter 6 presents a socio-relational understanding of identity. It draws on the work of Kathleen Wallace, who proposes a relational or network model of the self, and Charles Taylor's dialogical, moral self to support a richer conception of the person. This alternative framework is used to foreground deeper questions about the scope of consent-vitiating identity deceptions in law—questions that are explored in Part III.

The final three chapters present the three stages of the equivalence thesis. Chapter 7 presents the first stage (A) of the thesis through discussion of the law's approach to identity deception. This has the advantage of grounding the thesis in positive law, alongside attention to the implications for law and legal practice. Chapter 8 presents the second stage (B) of the thesis by means of a normative argument that identity deception should include impersonation of fictitious persons. This is developed through discussion of an important case: *R v Devonald*.[52] In parallel, analysis of the condition of 'personal knowing' in the impersonation provision is presented, and objections are addressed.

Chapter 9 presents the final stage (C) of the thesis, which argues that impersonation of a fictitious person is equivalent, morally speaking, to an individual pretending to be a different *kind* of person. This is the key move: it links qualitative with numerical identity deception. A Substantial Difference Argument is presented, which establishes the significance of deception about personal traits and attributes. Grounded in a socio-relational understanding of the self, this argument realises three objectives. First, it provides a justification for treating numerical and qualitative identity deception as morally equivalent. Second, it anticipates an objection that what is morally salient is actually *similarity* and not identity. Third, it sets some parameters around the potentially very wide scope of consent-vitiating identity deceptions by requiring *sufficient* change. By anchoring the qualitative with the numerical, it ensures the account is well grounded. Importantly, these parameters are set on a principled, not pragmatic, basis, which improves upon existing accounts limiting the scope of the law for unprincipled reasons.[53] Concluding remarks are

[52] [2008] EWCA Crim 527.

[53] This is particularly the case with deceptive sex. For example, Kennedy (2021); Williams (2008). A major

concern is over-criminalisation. Of course, the idea of 'over' is somewhat question-begging. If deceptive sex is, in an important sense, as bad as paradigmatic rape, the question of excessiveness does not arise.

provided in the final chapter, including a case study to bring the book's diverse elements together.

1.5 Assumptions and Definitions

The theoretical-philosophical literature on personal identity is extensive and richly diverse. Clarity is, therefore, required when using the concept. As a preliminary matter, it is necessary to distinguish between personal identity theory on the one hand, and identity and social identity theories on the other. Beyond the basic distinction drawn between roles and groups, these latter concepts are sometimes poorly differentiated in the literature. They offer two explanatory frameworks for understanding the social basis of the concept of the self and the nature of normative behaviour.[54] In brief, identity theory accounts for the relationship between the self and social structure, whereas social identity theory accounts for social identities. The most pertinent link in this book is with social identity. In later chapters, a socio-relational account of identity will bolster the book's thesis.

The concept of personal identity is distinct from several related concepts. These include: the 'persona' individuals may adopt as part of their self-presentation; the legal concept of 'personality', which is the totality of an entity's rights and duties recognised in law; and the concept of 'personhood,' which asks what makes people persons. Per Locke, human identity is distinguished from personal identity. The literature does not always clearly distinguish persons and selves. There is no consensus on the distinction, nor on the precise meaning of each term. The literature, most commonly, distinguishes persons as a unity or whole, while the self is variously described in terms of its relation to the whole. For example, per Greenwood, a self can refer to an integrated set of fundamental beliefs, attitudes, and desires.[55] Although I share this whole-part understanding, I will use self and person interchangeably where this reflects what is common in the literature and thus aids in clarity. However, I take no position on this debate.

A central distinction is between a numerical identity relation and a qualitative identity relation. Numerical identity concerns self-identity: it is the relation one thing bears to itself. It refers to an object that is 'one and the same object across time.'[56] This is diachronic sameness and is the basis for the concept's use in law. It is the type of identity that animates the personal identity problem. Qualitative identity concerns two or more objects sharing the same qualities or properties. This is synchronic sameness—to be the same person or thing at a single point in time. It is the property

[54] Hogg et al. (1995), p. 255.

[55] Greenwood (1994).

[56] Gligorov and Vitrano (2011), p. 148.

of being 'exactly alike'.[57] These are 'two kinds of sameness, of identity'.[58] The difference can be understood in terms of strict and non-strict identity, or identity and similarity, which appears in the empirical literature. As Lane explains,[59] strict identity requires exact sameness, whereas non-strict identity allows for some variation. Whether or not there is strict or non-strict identity depends on the nature of the object and its purposes.[60] In this book, use of the term 'numerical identity' (NI) will refer to 'numerical sameness of the psychological subject over time', and 'qualitative identity' (QI) will refer to 'qualitative sameness of psychological life.'[61] That is, the inner life of the person. Identity in the sense of psychological continuity[62] is not intended to foreclose further analytical features.

Section 76(2)(b) of the 2003 Act sets out the legal rule prohibiting identity deception. It employs the concept of identity in the numerical sense: the person with whom V subjectively agrees to have sex should be the person with whom V in fact has sex. In numerical identity terms, this can be explicated as: the person known personally at time t^1 should be the same person with whom V has sex at time t^2. This section will be referred to in places as the 'impersonation provision' for convenience. 'V' and 'D' are employed as shorthand for victims and defendants, respectively—with V denoting the woman who has been deceived and, D, the man who has deceived her. I focus on male sexual violence towards women given its statistical prevalence.

Cases

R v Devonald [2008] EWCA Crim 527
R v Melin [2019] EWCA Crim 557, [2019] QB 1063

References

Christman J (2004) Narrative unity as a condition of personhood. Metaphilosophy 35(5):695–713
Dennett D (1976) The conditions of personhood. In: Rorty A (ed) The identities of persons. University of California Press, Berkeley, pp 175–196
Eklund M (2004) Personal identity, concerns, and indeterminacy. Monist 87(4):489–511

[57] Parfit (1986).
[58] Ibid.
[59] Lane (2011).
[60] Ibid, 103.
[61] Schechtman (1994).
[62] At a minimum, per Parfit (1984), this criterion includes 'memories, attitudes and/or values.

Eklund M (2015) Intuitions, conceptual engineering, and conceptual fixed points. In: Daly C (ed) The Palgrave handbook of philosophical methods. London: Palgrave Macmillan UK, pp 363–385
Foster C, Herring J (2017) Identity, personhood and the law. Springer
Gallagher S, Marcel AJ (1999) The self in contextualized action. J Conscious Stud 6(4):4–30
Gligorov N, Vitrano C (2011) The impact of personal identity on advance directives. J Value Inq 45(2):147–158
Greenwood JD (1994) A sense of identity: prolegomena to a social theory of personal identity. J Theory Soc Behav 24(1):25–46
Haslanger SA (2012) Resisting reality: social construction and social critique. Oxford University Press, New York
Hogg MA, Terry DJ, White KM (1995) A tale of two theories: a critical comparison of identity theory with social identity theory. Soc Psychol Q 58(4):255–269
Kennedy C (2021) Criminalising deceptive sex: sex, identity and recognition. Leg Stud 41(1): 91–110
Korsgaard C (2003) Realism and constructivism in twentieth-century moral philosophy. J Philos Res 28(Supplement):99–122
Lane A (2011) The narrative self-constitution view: why Marya Schechtman cannot require it for personhood. Macalester J Philos 20(1):100–115
Locke J, Nidditch PH (1979) The clarendon edition of the works of John Locke: an essay concerning human understanding. Clarendon Press, New York
Moore MS (1985) The moral and metaphysical sources of the criminal law. In: Pennock R, Chapman JW (eds) Criminal justice, Nomos, vol 27. New York University Press, New York, pp 11–51
Moore MS (2013) Intention as a marker of moral culpability and legal punishment. In: Antony R, Green S (eds) Philosophical foundations of criminal law. Oxford University Press, Oxford, pp 179–205
Naffine N (2019) Criminal law and the man problem. Bloomsbury Publishing, Oxford
Norrie A (2014) Crime, reason and history: a critical introduction to criminal law, 3rd edn. Cambridge University Press, Cambridge
Olson E (1997) The human animal. Oxford University Press, Oxford
Otsuka M (1994) Killing the innocent in self-defense. Philos Public Aff 23(1):74–94
Parfit D (1984) Reasons and persons. Clarendon Press, Oxford
Parfit D (1986) Reasons and persons. Clarendon Press, Oxford
Perry J (1972) Can the self divide? J Philos 69(16):463–488
Plunkett D (2015) Which concepts should we use?: Metalinguistic negotiations and the methodology of philosophy. Inquiry 58(7-8):828–874
Reid T (1865) Essays on the intellectual powers of man, new edn. Griffin, London
Schechtman M (1994) The same and the same: two views of psychological continuity. Am Philos Q 31(3):199–212
Schechtman M (2014) Staying alive: personal identity, practical concerns, and the unity of a life. Oxford University Press, Oxford
Schechtman M (2018) The constitution of selves. Cornell University Press, Ithaca
Shoemaker D (2021) Personal identity and ethics. In: Zalta EN (ed) The Stanford encyclopedia of philosophy, Fall edn https://plato.stanford.edu/archives/fall2021/entries/identity-ethics/
Sider T (2001) Criteria of personal identity and the limits of conceptual analysis. Philos Perspect 15: 189–209
Strawson G (2004) Against narrativity. Ratio 17(4):428–452
Tadros V (2008) The scope and grounds of responsibility. New Criminal Law Review 11(1): 91–118
Taylor C (1992) Sources of the self: the making of modern identity. Cambridge University Press, Cambridge

Thomasson AL (2016) Conceptual ethics and the work of metaphysics. Microsoft Word - Thomasson.docx (unc.edu)

Tobia K (ed) (2022) Experimental philosophy of identity and the self, 1st edn. London, Bloomsbury Academic

Velleman DJ (2002) Motivation by ideal. Philos Explor 5(2):89–103

Wallace K (2019) The network self: relation, process, and personal identity. Routledge

West C (2009) Personal identity, conceptual analysis and no-fault disagreement. In: Vanderbeeken R, D'hooghe B (eds) Worldviews, science and us: studies of analytical metaphysics: A selection of topics from a methodological perspective. World Scientific Publishing Company, Singapore, pp 87–106

Williams RA (2008) Deception, mistake and vitiation of the victim's consent. Law Q Rev 124:132–159

Part I
Law's Problem with Identity

Chapter 2
Persons and the Law

2.1 Introduction

Identity is an important philosophical, social, and legal-political notion. This part of the book addresses its significance as a legal notion. Except for some reference to European Convention on Human Rights (ECHR) jurisprudence, discussion is limited to the law of England and Wales. Assuming that identity is a construct that is both fluid and static, the question arises as to its meaning in the legal context. The lack of a clear definition of identity in law has been observed.[1] Understanding the relation between law and identity requires, as a preliminary step, exploration of law's understanding of the concept of a person. In what follows, I provide an overview of this understanding through analysis of several areas in which the concept is salient, including contract, medical decision-making, crime, and ECHR jurisprudence. What emerges is a picture of its rich and multi-faceted nature, alongside the challenges and opportunities it poses for theorists wishing to make use of the concept.

2.2 Why Identity Matters

The concept of personal identity is of fundamental importance in law, as in other institutional systems. Having a stable notion of personal identity in terms of the continuity of persons is essential for determining personal responsibility, in both civil and criminal law. As Moore notes in his discussion of the criminal law, the law presupposes a certain view of persons as rational and autonomous and to this extent has a metaphysical basis.[2] For example, intuitions about intertemporal

[1] Bently (2010).

[2] Moore (1985).

R. Farah, *Rereading Identity Deception in the UK Sexual Offences Act 2003*,
SpringerBriefs in Law, https://doi.org/10.1007/978-3-031-44475-3_2

connectedness help to explain limitation statutes.[3] Perceived moral improvement can also explain favourable attitudes towards granting parole,[4] and whether a defendant is a different person can affect intuitions about how much punishment is deserved.[5] Furthermore, it is intimately bound up with ethical questions. Our moral practices presuppose a certain commitment to personal identity, even if not a specific ontology. Thus, unity of identity explains our blaming practices and our taking accountability for wrongs.

Personal identity is also an important concept in positive law. According to Marshall, much of human rights law can be related to personal identity: 'Indeed, one could argue that all ultimately derive from the importance of a person's identity in some sense.'[6] Such importance implies the right to establish the details of one's identity as an individual human being,[7] including in birth certificates and other records.[8] A right to identity is understood to have emerged out of the European Court of Human Rights' development of Article 8,[9] which protects the right to respect for private and family life. This has had implications, inter alia, for children born through international surrogacy arrangements and for transgender persons seeking legal recognition of their gender. Children born through international surrogacy have a stand-alone right to identity, provided chiefly through the Convention on the Rights of the Child and developed through the case law.[10] In rejecting the 'Corbett' test for determining a person's legal sex, the Court in *I v UK*[11] noted several important factors. Among these was 'the assumption by the transsexual of the social role of the assigned gender'.[12] This is a nod to the idea of social identities. An underexplored aspect of this decision was thus the salience of social reality in identity formation. Indeed, in its protection of Article 8 of the ECHR, the Court outlined the parameters of the concept of private life, explaining that, 'It can sometimes embrace aspects of an individual's physical and social identity'.[13]

---

[3]Tobia (2022), p. 2.

[4]Gomez-Lavin and Prinz (2019).

[5]Tobia (2022), p. 2.

[6]Marshall (2014), pp. 8–9.

[7]*Goodwin v UK* (2002) 35 EHRR 18 [90]; *I v UK* [2002] 2 FLR 518 [70]; *Mikulić v. Croatia*, no. 53176/99, § 54, ECHR 2002-I.

[8]*Goodwin*, ibid, in which the applicant sought legal recognition of her post-operative sex or gender identity.

[9]Marshall (2014), p. 36.

[10]For example, Articles 7 and 8 of the Convention on the Rights of The Child (CRC) 1989. The right to identity is broadly conceived, including a name, birth registration, nationality, and family relations. Continuity in ethnic, religious, cultural and linguistic background is provided for under Article 20 CRC. The leading cases are Mennesson v France, App. No 65192/11; Labassée v. France, App. No 65941/11.

[11]*I* (n 7).

[12]Ibid [81].

[13]Ibid [61]. See also *Mikulić* (n 7).

Personal identity is especially salient in life and death issues in morality and in law. The question of whether and when a fetus becomes a person is the perennial issue in the abortion debate. Asymmetry in moral status between the foetus and the would-be mother in caesarean section cases reflects the law's understanding of what it means to be a person.[14] It is the pivotal question in matters of medical decision-making in the context of assisted dying. Thus, in *Pretty v United Kingdom*,[15] the Court noted people's general concern 'that they should not be forced to linger on in old age or in states of advanced physical or mental decrepitude which conflict with strongly held ideas of self and personal identity.'[16] Provision for people to make advance directives in case of severe neurological decline reflects everyday judgments about identity change. Indeed, where patients request to end life-sustaining treatment due to a severely disabling (physical) condition,[17] we might understand such conditions as identity altering.

Some psychiatric disorders may also be identity altering.[18] The case law addressing anorexia nervosa (AN) illustrates this idea, as theorists have articulated a number of aspects of identity which are altered in AN.[19] Therefore, courts deciding whether advance decisions made by anorexics should be given legal effect may face what Coggon describes as 'a Parfitian metaphysical quandary.'[20] *A Local Authority* v *E*[21] is a case in point. This case concerned whether an anorexic should be given life-sustaining treatment in the form of forcible feeding against her wishes. Having found that *E* lacked capacity, the remaining question was whether the treatment would be in her best interests, having regard to her beliefs and values.[22] Peter Jackson J articulated the crux of the matter thus: 'It depends upon the assessment of her true identity. Has she been ill for so long that her illness would remain part of who she is, even if she had capacity? Or is she still *the person* she was before anorexia took its grip?'[23] This reflects the phenomenon of 'egosyntonicity,' whereby the disease is experienced as a part of the self.[24] Accordingly, if psychiatric conditions can be identity altering, then not disclosing a relevant condition to a sexual partner could come within identity deception, which lends further support to this book's thesis.

---

[14]For example, *St George's Healthcare National Health Service Trust v S* [1998] 2 WLR 936.

[15](2002) 35 EHRR 1.

[16]Application no. 2346/02, Council of Europe: European Court of Human Rights, 29 April 2002, available at: https://www.refworld.org/cases,ECHR,4dae1682.html [65].

[17]For example, *Ms B v An NHS Hospital Trust* [2002] 2 All ER 449.

[18]Hope (1994). See also Tan et al. (2003), p. 534.

[19]See, for example, Tan et al. (2003); Winston (2005); McAdams and Krawczyk (2014).

[20]Coggon (2013), p. 123.

[21][2012] EWHC 1639 (COP) [2012] HRLR 29.

[22]*Per* the Mental Capacity Act 2005, s 4(6).

[23]*E* (n 21) [78]. Emphasis added.

[24]Tan et al. (2003), p. 535.

2.3 Core Versus Attributes: A Persistent Problem?

As the above discussion shows, identity is a complex and multi-faceted concept. Perhaps because it has intrapsychic, interpersonal, and social dimensions,[25] consensus on its persistence conditions remains elusive. A further difficulty is the lack of clarity on what counts as the core of identity versus its attributes. Some personal identity theorists attempt to isolate core features, such as psychology,[26] or values.[27] Others doubt the existence of a core at all. Thus, social interactionist Gergen states, 'We don't seem to have a single, stable conception of ourselves... but to have the capacity for infinite fluctuation.'[28] And Oshana notes that few theorists of the self 'insist upon an immutable core, metaphysical or even metaphorical, upon which the essence of the self rests.'[29]

The criminal law has encountered similar difficulty. In discussing the line between lawful and unlawful sexual deceptions, the court in *R (Monica) v DPP*[30] noted the difficulty with the concept of identity. Citing *R v Clarence*,[31] the judge concurred that, 'There may be subtle metaphysical distinctions... between "identity", "attributes" and "qualities".'[32] Having made this observation, the Court declined to draw any fine distinctions and fell back on its broad bush approach. In particular, the Court was concerned to avoid bringing such behaviours as bigamy and seduction within the scope of rape. Allowing its reasoning to be guided by 'very subtle metaphysical distinctions' would lead to a line-drawing problem in both a conceptual and practical sense.[33] *R v Melin*[34] subsequently moved the law forward in the area of deception, endorsing a conception of personal identity that embraced certain of its qualitative aspects. While expanding the concept of identity, the Court limited it to status attributes integral to D's identity.[35] The potential for a more ambitious approach was thereby forestalled. This case is discussed in more detail in the next chapter.

Similar differentiation problems arise in the civil law context. Bently points to mistaken identity in contract law.[36] This doctrine can be understood as drawing a distinction between numerical and qualitative identity. Thus, *Lewis v Averay*[37]

---

[25] Ibid, p. 535.

[26] Unger (1990).

[27] Hitlin (2003); See also Hitlin (2011).

[28] Gergen in McGarty and Haslam (1996).

[29] Oshana (2010), p. 20.

[30] [2018] EWHC 3508 (QB).

[31] [1888] 22 QBD 23.

[32] *Monica* (n 30) [82].

[33] Ibid, [52].

[34] [2019] EWCA Crim 557, [2019] QB 1063.

[35] Ibid. [31].

[36] Bently (2010), p. 52.

[37] [1972] 1 QB 198.

established that only 'true mistakes as to identity', rather than mistakes as to attributes, can ground an action in mistake of identity. In identifying the nature of the mistake in such cases, the court will ask what the innocent party was centrally interested in. This is the indicator of what is of fundamental importance to the contract.[38] Thus, in *King's Norton Metal Co v Edridge Merrett & Co*,[39] it was the attribute of creditworthiness that was salient rather than the (numerical) identity of the company. A similar rationale is available in the criminal (sexual offences) case of *R v Linekar*,[40] in which what truly mattered to V was that D was validly "contracting" with her—that he was the bona fide client he claimed to be, and not whether he was Mr. Smith or Mr. Jones. In an important parallel for our purposes, creation of a fictitious identity in the law of contract is treated as deception as to attributes, not identity.[41] This does not leave the innocent party without recourse. But the action lies in fraudulent misrepresentation, not in mistake. As a doctrinal matter, the distinction is reflected in the fact that a contract is *void* in the former instance and *voidable* in the latter.[42] Perhaps, then, in sexual offences, rather than having no recourse for qualitative identity deception, it could be addressed through an evidential presumption, per s. 75 of the SOA.

There is judicial opposition to the afore-mentioned dichotomy. Senior judges have questioned whether it is meaningful to draw such 'fine distinctions,'[43] given the 'equivocal nature of a man's "identity".'[44] It has been described as 'A distinction without a difference'.[45] In *Averay,* Lord Denning captured the conceptual difficulty thus: 'A man's very name is one of his attributes. It is also a key to his identity.'[46] While this appears to support the idea of identity as equivocal, we could also interpret Lord Denning as highlighting an important *indicator* of identity. Thus, he could be distinguishing between the question of what identity is, versus how to determine it. Nevertheless, elsewhere, like Moore's scepticism about abstract metaphysical theorising,[47] it has been suggested that we are ill-advised to employ such distinctions in law.[48] In sum, this judicial response mirrors the trend in the literature towards a more nuanced approach to personal identity capable of reflecting its social reality. As will be seen in Part II, some theorists argue that the division between

---

[38] *Cundy v Lindsay* (1878) 3 app cas 459.

[39] (1897) 14 TLR 98.

[40] [1995] 2 CAR 49.

[41] *King's Norton* (n 39).

[42] That a contract is void not voidable in mistake as to identity was explicitly confirmed in *Shogun Finance Ltd v Hudson* [2003] UKHL 62 [48] (Lord Hobhouse for the Majority).

[43] *Averay* (n 37) (Lord Denning).

[44] *Shogun* (no 42) [59] (Lord Millett).

[45] *Averay* (n 37).

[46] Ibid.

[47] Moore (1985), p. 11.

[48] *Shogun* (n 42) (Lord Nicholls). See also Moore (ibid) for scepticism.

identity and similarity—between numerical identity and qualitative identity—is less sharp than assumed.

2.4 Conclusion

Personal identity is a complex and multi-faceted concept. The law's treatment of identity reflects this complexity. There are recurrent themes, including debates around the core and peripheral features of identity, the emergence of a human right to identity, and the challenges posed by identity-altering conditions affecting people in the medical law context. Recent literature on the importance of qualitative aspects of personal identity is reflected in the legal domain. The question of the persistence conditions for identity is thus highly relevant in law, and is not merely of abstract, metaphysical interest.

Cases

Mennesson v France, App. No 65192/11
Labassée v. France, App. No 65941/11
King's Norton Metal Co v Edridge Merrett & Co (1897) 14 TLR 98
Cundy v Lindsay (1878) 3 app cas 459
Lewis v Averay [1972] 1 QB 198
R v Linekar [1995] 2 CAR 49
Shogun Finance Ltd v Hudson [2003] UKHL 62
Goodwin v UK (2002) 35 EHRR 18
I v UK [2002] 2 FLR 518
Mikulić v Croatia, no. 53176/99, § 54, ECHR 2002-I
Pretty v United Kingdom (2002) 35 EHRR 1
R v Clarence [1888] 22 QBD 23
R (Monica) v Director of Public Prosecutions [2018] EWHC 3508 (QB)
St George's Healthcare National Health Service Trust v S [1998] 2 WLR 936
Ms. B v An NHS Hospital Trust [2002] 2 All ER 449
A Local Authority v E [2012] EWHC 1639 (COP) [2012] HRLR 29
Re E (Medical Treatment: Anorexia) [2012] EWHC 1639 (COP), [2012] MHLO 55
R v Melin [2019] EWCA Crim 557, [2019] QB 1063

Legislation

Sexual Offences Act 2003, s. 76(2)(b)
The Mental Capacity Act 2005, s 4(6)
Convention on the Rights of the Child (CRC)

References

Bently L (2010) Identity and the law. In: Walker G, Leedham-Green E (eds) Identity: the Darwin College lectures. Cambridge University Press, Cambridge

Coggon J (2013) Anorexia nervosa, best interests, and the human right to 'a wholesale overwhelming of her autonomy': a Local Authority v E [2012] EWHC 1639 (COP) [2012] HRLR 29. Med Law Rev 22(1):119–130

Gergen KJ (1996) Social psychology as social construction: the emerging vision. In: McGarty C, Haslam S (eds) The message of social psychology: perspectives on mind in society. Blackwell, Oxford

Gomez-Lavin J, Prinz J (2019) Parole and the moral self: moral change mitigates responsibility. J Moral Educ 48(1):65–83

Hitlin S (2003) Values as the core of personal identity: drawing links between two theories of self. Soc Psychol Q 66:118–137

Hitlin S (2011) Values, personal identity, and the moral self. In: Schwartz SJ, Luyckx K, Vignoles VL (eds) Handbook of identity theory and research, vol 2. Springer, New York, pp 515–529

Hope T (1994) Personal identity and psychiatric illness. R Inst Philos Suppl 37:131–143

Marshall J (2014) Human rights law and personal identity. Routledge, pp 8–9

McAdams CJ, Krawczyk DC (2014) Who am I? How do I look? Neural differences in self-identity in anorexia nervosa. Soc Cogn Affect Neurosci 9(1):12–21

Moore MS (1985) The moral and metaphysical sources of the criminal law. In: Pennock R, Chapman JW (eds) Criminal justice. Nomos XXVII. New York University Press, New York, pp 11–51

Oshana MA (2010) Self and identity. In: The importance of how we see ourselves: self-identity and responsible agency, Blue Ridge Summit. Lexington Books/Fortress Academic, pp 19–53

Tan PJ, Jacinta OA, Hope T, Stewart A (2003) Anorexia nervosa and personal identity: the accounts of patients and their parents. Int J Law Psychiatry 26(5):533–548

Tobia K (ed) (2022) Experimental philosophy of identity and the self, 1st edn. Bloomsbury Academic, London

Unger P (1990) Identity, consciousness and value. Oxford University Press, Incorporated, New York

Winston AP (2005) Projection, introjection and identity in anorexia nervosa. Br J Psychother 21(3): 389–399

Chapter 3
Identity in Sexual Offences Law

3.1 Introduction

How does the Sexual Offences Act 2003 construct personal identity as it relates to deceptive sex? This chapter briefly sets out the legal context, namely the law's treatment of sexual autonomy as the animating ideal of sexual offences law. It summarises other attempts to strengthen protection against deceptive sex and discusses *R v Melin.*[1] Although this case concerned an offence against the person, it moved the law forward in false representation as to identity, albeit stopping short of a more generous reading of the concept of identity.

3.2 The (Mis)Treatment of Sexual Autonomy

The Sexual Offences Act 2003 was passed following the Home Office report: *Setting the Boundaries: Reforming the Law on Sex Offences.*[2] Despite this report presenting the protection of sexual autonomy as the master principle or value that any sexual offences law should uphold,[3] in practice it is radically qualified.[4] The failure of consent is also widely observed.[5] Courts routinely fail to protect autonomy as a subjective matter, such that many deceptions affirmed by victims as critical to their

[1] [2019] EWCA 557 (Crim), [2019] QB 1063.

[2] Home Office, *Setting the Boundaries: Reforming the Law on Sex Offences* (Summary Report and Recommendations, Vol 1, 2000).

[3] Ibid, para 2.7.2.

[4] For example, Rubenfeld (2012); Schulhofer (1998).

[5] For example, Herring (2014); Tadros (2006); Munro (2014).

R. Farah, *Rereading Identity Deception in the UK Sexual Offences Act 2003*, SpringerBriefs in Law, https://doi.org/10.1007/978-3-031-44475-3_3

consent are ignored. These include career or worldview,[6] marital status,[7] fertility status,[8] age and wealth.[9] In *R (Monica) v DPP*,[10] for example, it did not matter that the victim (V)'s core beliefs in environmental activism and 'radical, street protest'[11] were a central part of her identity and she had exercised her sexual autonomy on the understanding that these were shared with the defendant (D). Certainly, 'disingenuous blandishments of or common or garden lies'[12] are deemed too trivial, too peripheral, to give rise to evidential or conclusive presumptions.[13] There is a consensus that 'acute difficulties'[14] persist in addressing deceptive sex.

The difficulty posed by deception was demonstrated most recently in *R v Lawrance.*[15] This case concerned an active deception about the fundamental matter of fertility. Yet, the conviction for rape was overturned on the basis that fertility did not go to the act itself but merely to its broader circumstances. Thus, V's sexual autonomy was overridden via an artificial distinction between deception relating to the sexual act versus the 'quality of the ejaculate and the potential consequences and risks associated with it'.[16] This reveals an implicitly male-centric approach. For the man, the fertility causing effects do not impact on his experience of the physical act. For a fertile woman, the physical act includes its fertility-causing features. By splitting off the action from its proximate effects, and despite those effects being the subject of a condition, it privileged the male experience. As a matter of consistency, the court would seem required to endorse the following absurd implication: that a man who lied about a vasectomy, which is to make a claim about the quality of ejaculate, cannot be guilty of rape; while a man who lied about his very ability to ejaculate, could be guilty of rape because this is to make a claim about the act itself.[17] This is so despite both Ds having secured V's consent by claiming to meet her condition that there be no (or negligible) risk of pregnancy. It is unsatisfactory that the particular tactic D uses to trick V should make all the difference in terms of whether consent is vitiated. Under the approach endorsed in this book, fertility would be an aspect of D's identity about which V has a right to know.

---

[6] *R (Monica) v DPP* [2018] EWHC 3508 (Admin), [2019] QB 1019.

[7] *Papadimitropoulos v The Queen* [1957] HCA 74; 98 CLR 249.

[8] *R v Lawrance* [2020] EWCA Crim 971, [2020] 2 Cr App R 29.

[9] Traits and attributes such as age, wealth, marital status, declarations of love ruled out, *obiter*, in cases such as *R v McNally* [2013] EWCA Crim 1051, [2014] 1 QB 593.

[10] *Monica* (n 6).

[11] Ibid, [36].

[12] *Jheeta* [2007] EWCA Crim 1699 [24] (Sir Igor Judge), [2008] 1 WLR 2582.

[13] SOA 2003, ss 75 and 76, respectively.

[14] *Lawrance* (n 8).

[15] Ibid.

[16] Ibid, [19].

[17] Equally, condom removal and sabotage can ground a rape conviction. See, respectively: Assange v Swedish Prosecution Authority [2011] EWHC 2849 (Admin); R v Hutchinson 2014 SCC 19, [2014] S.C.R. 346.

The academic literature is replete with strategies for better protecting women from sexual harm. Herring has advocated an unqualified right to autonomy in respect of mistaken consent (and *a fortiori*, deception).[18] This places emphasis on the victim's perspective and her right to absolute respect for the conditions she places on consent. This is so even where those conditions are based on personal prejudice.[19] Thus, Herring states '[V] is under no duty to supply sexual service to others on a non-discriminatory basis.'[20] Other proposals seek to balance the interests of victims against the countervailing interests of defendants or public policy goals.[21] For example, in the context of mistake, Gardner has proposed a combined subjective-objective assessment of the significance of mistakes giving rise to consent.[22] As Herring observes, this approach risks imposing a Western secular perspective of sex and sexual ethics, which fails to respect the views of minority religious and cultural groups.[23] Such failure is not trivial. Dan-Cohen calls attention to this issue in his discussion of a dignity principle for the criminal law.[24] He identifies a similar pretence of neutrality underpinning the harm principle, which is predominant in criminal law theory.[25] In proposing dignity as an alternative, he argues that this would accommodate cultural variation, among other advantages. In short, it is not for others to judge what victims ought to care about in relation to sex.

Some commentators treat the sexual autonomy interests of V and D as though they are on a par, morally speaking.[26] Yet, a person's right to positive sexual autonomy is simply not in issue when the other party does not consent; for the scope of the right does not cover sex with *non-consenting* persons. As Herring explains, "Respect for autonomy gives us a reason to leave someone alone so that they can live the life they wish. It does not require us to fulfil everyone's desires.' Thus, the principle of autonomy prevents only those exercises which *unjustifiably* harm another'.[27] Another way to put this is that the positive aspect of the right to sexual autonomy is exercisable against the state, that is, vertically, and not against prospective sexual partners. Assuming moral equivalence between V and D also underestimates the constraining effect of male dominance on female autonomy.[28]

In view of this inadequate situation, this book takes a novel approach that brings out the latent potential of the impersonation provision in the 2003 Act.[29] Noting the

[18] Herring (2005).
[19] Dougherty (2013).
[20] Herring (2022), p. 471.
[21] Dyer (2019); Horder (1999); Pattinson (2009); Williams (2008).
[22] Gardner (1996), p. 288.
[23] Herring (2021), p. 58.
[24] Dan-Cohen (2009).
[25] Ibid.
[26] Rubenfeld (2012).
[27] Herring (2022), p. 471.
[28] Friedman (2004).
[29] SOA 2003, s 76(2)(b).

Court's recognition in *Lawrance* that 'any novel circumstances must be considered by reference to the statutory definition' in the 2003 Act,[30] it takes up this challenge directly by looking at the statute itself. The approach is, moreover, inspired by Herring's 2005 article on mistaken consent, in which he suggested that s. 76(2)(a) of the Act could be read more broadly.[31]

3.3 The Impersonation Provision

Conclusive presumptions about consent are found in s. 76 of the 2003 Act. This 'impersonation provision' requires that 'the defendant intentionally induced the complainant to consent to the relevant act by impersonating a person known personally to the complainant'.[32] Where deception is deemed not to fall under s. 76, consent may still be vitiated under the general definition of consent under s. 74, which states that "... a person consents if he agrees by choice, and has the freedom and capacity to make that choice." Where s. 76 is satisfied, this is conclusive evidence of no consent and both the *mens rea* and the *actus reus* of rape are proved.[33] Accordingly, an active deception is necessary (though not sufficient).[34] Where a defendant merely takes advantage of V's unilateral mistake, as in *R v Elbekkay*,[35] this is dealt with under s. 74.

The impersonation provision carries a personal acquaintance requirement. Although the meaning of this element is not entirely clear, it plausibly rules out indirect knowledge/experience of the object of the impersonation. V must normally have met or encountered him or her in some sense. This rules out famous persons and historical figures of which one's experience is second-hand. The 'person' requirement seems to exclude fictitious persons, as in *R v Devonald*.[36] Plausibly, the section also requires that the deception is *effective* in causing V to consent.[37] The section does not mention causation, so it is open to argument that consent under mere circumstances of deception is sufficient for liability. However, not only is this implausible, but the problem can be solved through a proper reading of the word 'inducement'—implying success in bringing about a desired outcome.

[30] *Lawrance* (n 8) [42].
[31] Herring (2005).
[32] SOA 2003, s 76(2)(b).
[33] Herring (2022), p. 417.
[34] See *Lawrance* (n 8).
[35] [1995] Crim LR 163 (CA).
[36] [2008] EWCA Crim 527.
[37] A view supported by Herring (2022), pp. 417–418.

3.4 *R v Melin*[38]

The law draws a sharp line drawn between identity, on the one hand, and traits/ attributes, on the other.[39] But in *Melin,* the court accepted that although deception as to a person's qualifications could not *generally* vitiate consent,[40] attributes that were 'inextricably linked' to a person's professional status could form part of his or her identity and thereby vitiate consent.[41] Moreover, it would not need to be shown that this changed the nature of the act. Crucially, the Court embraced a definition of identity as 'the fact of being who *or what* a person is'.[42] This broadened identity beyond its numerical ('who') aspect. As noted by Pegg and Thomas, 'who and what a person is may be very different'.[43] Furthermore, *Melin* recognised that attributes could be more important than identity in certain situations, such that the trait may be the defining feature of one's identity. *R v Linekar*[44] seems to make sense on this interpretation; it is conceivable that V would have preferred sex with an imposter who was willing to pay her for the sexual act rather than sex with D who was not.

Despite this case moving the law forward, it is both circumscribed and ambiguous in several respects. First, it only applies to status attributes, and then only where said attribute is 'integral to his identity'.[45] This seems to guard both against 'trivial lies'[46] and purportedly trivial professions—a familiar judicial rejoinder in such cases. Yet, when we ask *for whom* it is integral, it seems not to matter what the individual victim thinks. This position is curious, given that it departs from the treatment in other areas of law. Indeed, Simler J cited approvingly text from Smith and Hogan's Criminal Law in which the authors ask what *the patient* is most concerned about.[47] In relation to informed consent in medical practice, *Montgomery v Lanarkshire Health Board*[48] established that material risks include risks that matter to the patient.[49] Furthermore, Simler J endorsed the reasoning in *R v Richardson*, according to which 'it is the nature of the mistake as to consent that is relevant and not the reason why the mistake has been made'.[50] In doing so, she recognised the subjective viewpoint of the victim. Yet, the case does not give full effect to that viewpoint, given that a positive deception that goes to one's 'professional position or standing' also seems required.[51]

[38] [2019] EWCA Crim 557.

[39] See *Monica* (n 6); *Papadimitropoulos* (n 7).

[40] *R v Richardson* [1998] EWCA Crim 3269, [1998] 2 Cr App R 200.

[41] *Melin* (n 36) [30].

[42] Ibid [31]. Emphasis added.

[43] Pegg and Thomas (2019), p. 301.

[44] [1995] 2 Cr App R 49.

[45] *Melin* (n 36) [31].

[46] Ibid [29].

[47] Ormerod et al. (2018).

[48] [2015] UKSC 11, [2015] 1 AC 1430.

[49] Ibid [47] (Lord Kerr and Lord Reed).

[50] *Melin* (n 36) [28].

[51] Pegg and Thomas (2019).

The crux of the problem is that the 'what' of personal identity plausibly encompasses far more than *Melin* allows. A 'wide range of personal attributes, from personal beliefs and qualifications, to gender, marital status and religion'[52] may be considered integral. Williams notes the uncertainty about whether qualifications cases are best thought of as 'nature of the act' or as 'identity' deceptions.[53] In *R v Tabassum*,[54] the touching was exactly what was expected in the examination, yet the absence of medical qualifications changed the nature of the act consented to. Indeed, Pegg and Thomas theorise that the Court's approach to identity deceptions in *Melin* may, despite speaking in terms of attributes,[55] be a way of 'describing a fundamental matter which may go to the heart of the *nature* of the act'.[56] In some cases, the choice of paradigm will not make a difference. *McNally*,[57] although decided as a nature of the act case, also fits within an identity paradigm. But a post-operative defendant in a *McNally-type case* may be acquitted under a nature of the act analysis and found guilty under a suitably rich identity analysis. This is particularly so as the charge was one of digital penetration and not penile penetration, such that there would seem to be little difference between men and women.[58] This is so, notwithstanding the fact that there may be a prior question as to what terms such as 'male' and 'female' should be taken to mean, and people may reasonably disagree about the validity and usefulness of binary distinctions of this kind.[59]

Finally, based on *Melin*,[60] it is unclear whether the fact that a doctor had been struck off would go to his identity. Fitness to practice seems to be an attribute going to the heart of his status—for a doctor who is unfit to practice is, for all intents and purposes, not a doctor. In such a case, we would surely say it is not simply that he is unlicensed, as in *Richardson*,[61] but that he is undeserving of being called a doctor, thereby coming under *Melin*. Because he lacks 'professional position or standing',[62] he would not be accepted into a community of his peers. Importantly, this contains a hint of communitarianism about identity, which is addressed in Chap. 9.

---

[52] Ibid, p. 301.

[53] Williams (2008).

[54] [2000] Crim LR 686.

[55] Mirroring *Tabassum* (ibid) in this respect, despite its 'quality of the act' language.

[56] Pegg and Thomas (2019), p. 302.

[57] *McNally* (n 9). Although s 76 of the SOA 2003 was not invoked, deception as to gender identity vitiated consent on the facts.

[58] Although one might think that digital penetration as an alternative to penile penetration has symbolic significance and/or particular social meaning that differs relevantly between men and woman, and indeed, between heterosexual and homosexual relationships.

[59] For a critique of power and privilege in this context, see Sharpe (2017).

[60] *Melin* (n 36).

[61] *Richardson* (n 38) [55].

[62] Ibid.

3.5 Conclusion

The above discussion shows that this area of the law is ripe for re-exploring. While noting the ability of courts to incrementally expand the categories of legally operative deceptions,[63] a view that treats traits/attributes as standalone vitiating factors, suitably theorised, is to be preferred. This is especially appropriate in sexual relations where a shared attribute may be an identifying aspect of the parties' relationship.[64] This approach would resolve cases like *Monica* and *Papadimitropoulos* in the interests of the victims.[65] A key question will arise: 'When is an attribute integral to one's identity?' Parts II and III of this book answer this question by appeal to a richer account of identity. For the sake of argument, I set aside the more basic point that if we think that negative moral change in someone changes the identity core of that person, deception, in and of itself, could be identity determining.[66]

Reports

Home Office, *Setting the Boundaries: Reforming the Law on Sex Offences* (Summary Report and Recommendations, Vol 1, 2000)

Cases

R v Devonald [2008] EWCA Crim 527
R v Elbekkay [1995] Crim LR 163 (CA)
R v Hutchinson 2014 SCC 19, [2014] S.C.R. 346
Assange v Swedish Prosecution Authority [2011] EWHC 2849 (Admin)
Fagan v Metropolitan Police Commissioner [1968] EWHC 1 (QB), [1969] 1 QB 439
R v Jheeta [2007] EWCA Crim 1699, [2008] 1 WLR 2582, [2007] 2 Cr App R 34
R v Lawrance [2020] EWCA Crim 971, [2020] 2 Cr App R 29
R v Linekar [1995] 2 Cr App R 49
R v Melin [2019] EWCA 557 (Crim)
R v McNally [2013] EWCA Crim 1051
R (Monica) v DPP [2018] EWHC 3508 (Admin), [2019] QB 1019

---

[63] See proposals from Dyer (2019); Williams (2008).

[64] Herring in conversation, 2020.

[65] Subject, in addition, to resolving the question of intentional inducement. Arguably, the 'continuing act' doctrine could be applied to this end. See *Fagan v Metropolitan Police Commissioner* [1968] EWHC 1 (QB), [1969] 1 QB 439.

[66] This was the finding in a recent study looking at children's concept of personal identity: Košová et al. (2021), p. 75.

Montgomery v Lanarkshire Health Board [2015] UKSC 11, [2015] 1 AC 1430
Papadimitropoulos v The Queen [1957] HCA 74; 98 CLR 249
R v Richardson [1998] EWCA Crim 3269, [1998] 2 Cr App R 200
R v Tabassum [2000] Crim LR 686

Legislation

Sexual Offences Act 2003, s. 76(2)(b)
Offences Against the Person Act 1861

References

Dan-Cohen M (2009) Harmful thoughts: essays on law, self, and morality. Princeton University Press
Dougherty T (2013) Sex, lies, and consent. Ethics 123:717–744
Dyer A (2019) Mistakes that negate apparent consent. Crim Law J 43:159–179
Friedman M (2004) Autonomy and male dominance. Soundings: an Interdisciplinary Journal 87(1/2):175–200
Gardner S (1996) Appreciating Olugboja. Leg Stud 16:275–297
Herring J (2005) Mistaken sex. Crim Law Rev 2005:511–524
Herring J (2014) Rape and the definition of consent. Natl Law Sch India Rev 26:62
Herring J (2021) Consent mistaken. In: Reforming the relationship between sexual consent, deception, and mistake. Criminal Law Reform Now Network. http://www.clrnn.co.uk/publications-reports/
Herring J (2022) Criminal law: text, cases and materials, 10th edn. Oxford University Press, Oxford
Horder J (1999) Consent, threats and deception in criminal law. King's Law J 10(1):104–108
Košová MJ et al (2021) My friend's true self: children's concept of personal identity. Philos Psychol 34(1):47–75
Munro V (2014) Sexual autonomy. In: Markus D Dubber and Tatjana Hörnle (eds) The Oxford handbook of criminal law. Oxford, OUP, pp 747–767
Ormerod D, Smith JC, Laird K (2018) Smith, Hogan, and Ormerod's criminal law. Oxford University Press
Pattinson SD (2009) Consent and informational responsibility. J Med Ethics 35(3):176–179
Pegg S, Thomas M (2019) Deception and qualifications: revisiting the ruling in R v Richardson? J Crim Law 83(4):298–303
Rubenfeld J (2012) The riddle of rape-by-deception and the myth of sexual autonomy. Yale Law J 122:1372
Schulhofer S (1998) Unwanted sex: the culture of intimidation and the failure of law. Harvard University Press, Cambridge
Sharpe A (2017) The ethicality of the demand for (trans)parency in sexual relations. Aust Fem Law J 43(2):161–183
Tadros V (2006) Rape without consent. Oxf J Leg Stud 26(3):515–543
Williams R (2008) Deception, mistake and vitiation of victim's consent. Law Q Rev 124:132–159

Chapter 4
Deception as to Identity: Three Rationales

4.1 Introduction

In arguing that the law on deception as to identity should include qualitative aspects, the motivating idea is that numerical identity is simply not all that matters in impersonation-type cases. In focusing on numerical identity alone, the law forecloses the opportunity to develop a richer sexual offences law and a more sophisticated account of identity-related harms—one that reflects the importance of identity to people's subjective judgments in exercising their sexual autonomy. To put pressure on the law's position, this chapter explores the underlying rationale of the impersonation provision. Beyond the idea of wrongs and harms, criminal law scholarship does not address this in any depth. However, it is possible to say more. At least, I will attempt to do so.

In what follows, three rationales are considered. I argue that it is possible to identify these rationales, even though they are unstated in the law. The aim is to show that each rationale that is hypothesised to underlie numerical identity deception, carries over to qualitative identity deception. Although the third rationale does so less convincingly, it is, in any case, morally unappealing as a rationale.

4.2 Rationale 1: Relational Intimacy

> Prohibiting impersonation prevents D from taking advantage of relational intimacy to weaken or bypass consent.

In sexual relationships marked by familiarity, affection and mutual concern (relational intimacy), consent may not be morally salient. As Chamallas observes, the appropriate description of sexual relations within a couple is not that the woman

R. Farah, *Rereading Identity Deception in the UK Sexual Offences Act 2003*, SpringerBriefs in Law, https://doi.org/10.1007/978-3-031-44475-3_4

consented to it, but that the parties were mutually desiring actors in it.[1] Thus, *wantedness* or *mutuality* may be a better notion, and both have been proposed as ways to reform or displace the consent model. Building on Chamallas' view, I suggest that in romantic relationships there are general reasons (though defeasible) to engage in sexual intimacy with one's partner.[2] In such relationships, the parties cultivate a 'reservoir' of emotional and relational capital. This provides the context for sexual interaction, from which D benefits illegitimately through impersonation. There are two possible ways of conceptualising this wrong. The first is as a type of exploitation, understood as wrongful gain.[3] This is defendant focused. It involves D benefiting from a reservoir that is not his. The second has to do with weakening a normative power. This is victim focused. It looks at the effect on V of D's claiming to satisfy her reason/s for having sex—for consenting. I will focus on the latter kind of wrong before considering the former. As will be seen, it is important to disambiguate the nature of the wrong at stake.

4.2.1 Qualitative Identity

Does the fact of relational intimacy justify prohibiting deception as to the type of person D is? The rationale does seem to carry over, though not straightforwardly, as follows. We need to consider what this reservoir does in terms of V's consent. Most obviously, what it does is supply V with general reasons, other things equal, to have sex with the particular person (whom D impersonates). Other things equal, persons in recognised intimate relationships engage in regular sexual activity with each other. This is so whether or not they also engage in sexual activity with others. This may be regular or irregular in terms of frequency. Indeed, such relationships may encounter difficulty. But assuming a standard intimate relationship marked by affection and mutual concern, it is reasonable to suppose that the parties take themselves to have a general reason to have sex with each other. Now, with qualitative identity deception (pretending to be a different kind of person), though D may not have this reservoir in the way that he does in numerical identity deception (pretending to be someone else), his deception has the same structure. In presenting himself as a different *kind* of person, he is responding to one or more reasons V has for having sex with *such a person.* Is this not analogous with someone whose relational intimacy with V provides her with such reasons? After all, in both cases, D is pretending to satisfy V's reasons.

---

[1] Chamallas (1987).

[2] I do not argue that there are general reasons to have sex *per se*. I endorse the view taken by Madden Dempsey and Herring (2007) and Wall (2015) that there are general reasons *against* sexual penetration. Here, I am making the more limited point that there are reasons in the context of an existing relationship of sexual intimacy.

[3] See Feinberg (1990); Mayer (2007).

The crux of this argument is the idea that relational-emotional capital cultivated within a romantic relationship, other things equal, is a proxy for there being general reasons to have sex (whenever there are reasons to have sex) *with each other*. It is the idea of there being relatively stable reasons in favour of consent to sex (with a particular person). Claiming to have *qualities* that appeal to V manifests this same structure. It is capable of supplying V with reasons to have sex (with a particular type of person). The aspect common to both is this influence upon V's reasons. In this respect, it is not clear why the mere fact that D impersonates a hypothetical person should mean that V is denied legal protection.

Superficially, the analogy may work. But we might ask whether these reasons differ in their quality, and if so, whether this is a morally relevant difference. In numerical identity deception, D claims to be the person with whom V has cultivated the reservoir. But in qualitative identity deception, D claims to be the kind of person with whom V *could* cultivate a reservoir (they may proceed to cultivate such a reservoir or have more minimal personal knowledge of each other). This latter form of deception thus provides V with reasons in a more remote fashion: D supplies V with reasons *to have reasons*. An example might help to illuminate the issue. Let's say that D has lied to V about being extremely wealthy. This fact is of crucial importance to V's consent. They go on to develop a sexual relationship. In the process of coming to know each other, D has genuinely cultivated relational and emotional capital with V, but he would not have been able to do so without his lie. *R (Monica) v DPP*[4] has this structure. In that case, D pretended to be an environmental activist. This enabled him to cultivate a seemingly genuine romantic connection with V, which ultimately led to a sexual relationship.

The decision in *Monica* shows that supplying V with reasons to have reasons is not the kind of deception the law cares about. At a minimum, D must supply V with reasons directly. The requirement that D's deception must induce V's consent reflects this. But I think we can challenge this view on two grounds. First, I suggested above that there were two ways of conceptualising the wrong. One was the effect on V of D's deception, and the other was D's wrongful gain in claiming the reservoir as his. The discussion so far has focused on the effect on V (on her reasons). But what if we focus instead on D? If the wrong to be prevented is the fact that D has unfairly benefited from such capital, the rationale would carry over. The law would simply say that D cannot benefit from a reservoir that belongs either to a different person or to a different kind of person.

Should the law of rape, and the impersonation provision specifically, be reorientated towards D? Some theorists have argued for a victim or women centred definition of rape. For example, MacKinnon criticises the way in which the law is orientated around accepted norms of male sexual behaviour, instead of a focus on what the victim suffers—her violation. An example of this is the mens rea standard under the general definition of consent, which requires D's reasonable belief and not,

[4] [2018] EWHC 3508 (Admin), [2019] QB 1019.

instead, asking what V reasonably conveyed.[5] The better view is to give due attention to what D did and intended. Asking, for example, whether D's lie was significant enough to V to count as unlawful is entirely the wrong question. In this vein, Herring has proposed that greater focus be given to D's actions and responsibility.[6] This would have implications for the impersonation provision, which requires that D *intend* that his deception induce V to consent. In *Monica*,[7] it was not enough that D intended his deception. Although he benefited from his deception, without which he could not have secured sex with V, he must have intended that it had the effect on V's consent. The decision in *Monica* tells us that it is not sufficient that D's deception created the *conditions* under which V consented. Yet, the law could equally have chosen to accept as sufficient Ds intentional deception, which is a but-for cause of V's consent, and D's knowledge (subjective or objective) that V would not otherwise have consented.[8] I argue in the next section that mens rea need not coincide in time with the initial positive act of deception.

The second basis on which to challenge the law's focus is by considering an analogy with homicide law. Involuntary manslaughter is an unlawful killing done without an intention to kill or to cause grievous bodily harm. It has the same structure as the offence of murder, except that death will have been caused either by D's unlawful or dangerous act, or gross negligence.[9] Applying this to impersonation, the offence could be formulated to require that D intentionally deceive V from which V's consent knowingly resulted. Now, deceit is not an unlawful or dangerous act, but an argument could be made that sexual deception (of the right kind) is an exploitative act, which could be treated as the base offence. Alternatively, a gross negligence argument also has promise if we think that consensual sexual relations imply a duty of care. At a minimum, where harm to V is reasonably foreseen, D is under a duty to care for V, foregoing his opportunity to take advantage of her.

Other areas of the criminal law provide additional support for my liability for omissions argument. Although there is not space to consider these in detail, I will briefly mention two: the *R v Miller*[10] 'creating a risk' doctrine and the *Fagan v Metropolitan Police Commissioner*[11] 'continuing act' doctrine.

In *Miller*, the defendant had inadvertently started a fire. His (knowing) failure to take steps to extinguish it resulted in the house catching fire. He was charged with arson under the Criminal Damage Act 1971, even though the fire was an accident and he had not undertaken any positive action in respect of it. The principle of law is that someone who negligently creates a risk is under a duty to take reasonable steps

[5] See Pineau (1989) for an argument that consent should be reformulated in terms of what is reasonable from a woman's point of view.

[6] Herring (2022); Gardner (1996) makes a similar point in respect of the law on manslaughter.

[7] *Monica* (n 4).

[8] See Herring (2005) for an argument related to mistaken consent.

[9] Homicide: Murder and Manslaughter | The Crown Prosecution Service (cps.gov.uk).

[10] [1983] 2 AC 161, [1983] 1 All ER 978, [1983] 2 WLR 539, (1983) 77 Cr App R 17 (HL).

[11] [1969] 1 QB 439 (DC).

to prevent harm to others, including to property.[12] *Fagan* resembles *Miller*. It covers creation of a dangerous situation that poses a reasonable risk to others. But unlike *Miller*, the defendant in this case was unaware that his conduct had created such risk. Nevertheless, once he became aware, he was under a duty to act. This doctrine addresses the correspondence principle in criminal law doctrine, which requires that acts reus and mens rea overlap in time. In this case, D's omission was treated as 'adopting' the act that he had earlier committed unintentionally. This then coincided with mens rea. For clarity, *Miller* requires negligent creation of risk, awareness, and failure to act. *Fagan* requires unintentional creation of a dangerous situation posing a reasonable risk and intentional failure to act. The 'continuing act' doctrine was applied more recently in *DPP v Santa Bermudez*,[13] in which there was a failure to disclose the risk of harm to a police officer searching D's pocket. It was held that D had created a dangerous situation by carrying exposed needles, and then failed in his duty to alert the police officer to the risk this posed.

Applying this to the issue at hand, there are two possible loci of risk creation in identity deception. First, sexual penetration itself carries the risk of (at least physical) harm to V.[14] A normative claim could be made that there are innumerable other risks, but physical injury, being an inescapable consequence of penetration, is sufficient. Second, D's deception itself can be understood as risk/danger creating. Indeed, all deception creates a risk that V will consent against her best interests. Thus, in *Monica*, D's deception gave V reasons for sex that did not actually apply to her. In a similar vein, Herring notes that D would cause serious harm to V if the consent he was relying on was defective.[15] Indeed, the 2003 Act recognises this in s 79(2), which considers penetration as a continuing act from entry to withdrawal. This places an obligation on D to withdraw as soon as consent becomes defective. If he does not do so, his mens rea at the time of penetration can be applied to his subsequent omission.[16] The New Zealand Privy Council case of *Kaitamaki v The Queen* is an example of this.[17] Assuming that sexual penetration is a prima facie wrong, this places an obligation on D to ensure that V's consent truly reflects her own determination of her best interests.[18] Seen this way, the idea of shared responsibility fails to recognise the different normative positions of V and D.

Alternatively, it can be resolved via *Fagan* in the following way. Although D did not intend for V to consent on the basis of his deception, we can treat his failure to prevent foreseeable harm to V as coinciding with his earlier intention to deceive V. *R v Lawrance*[19] can be similarly resolved. By analogy with *Miller*, D negligently

[12] Ashworth (1989), p. 439.

[13] [2003] EWHC 2908 (Admin).

[14] Madden Dempsey and Herring (2007).

[15] Herring (2021), pp. 55–56.

[16] Rape and Sexual Offences - Chapter 6: Consent | The Crown Prosecution Service (cps.gov.uk).

[17] [1985] AC 147.

[18] Herring (2021), p. 55.

[19] [2020] EWCA Crim 971, [2020] 2 Cr App R 29.

created a risk of pregnancy when he penetrated V. Not withdrawing at the point of ejaculation, foreseeing the possible consequences, was then a culpable omission. I suggest that so-called gender fraud cases can also be resolved in this manner. For the sake of argument, we can characterise some of these cases as deception as to (trans) identity and/or sexual orientation.[20] By analogy with *Miller*, and similarly with *Monica*, D may not intend for such deception to induce consent. More plausibly, D has valid reasons for not wanting to disclose trans identity, which may be wholly unrelated to V. But the structure of *Miller* is nevertheless present.

As the discussion of these cases shows, this rationale can be applied in a convincing manner to qualitative identity deceptions including trans status, fertility, career or ideological identity, and so on. To come back to the initial point: I suggest that giving V reasons to have reasons *can* come within identity deception. I have argued that it is too demanding to require that the deception cause V's consent. Rather, it is sufficient that it is risk/danger-creating and D intentionally fails to prevent harm to V. In suggesting that D has a duty to act to prevent resulting harm to V, what this duty should entail is a question worth exploring. It might include disclosing a relevant fact to V, or starting a conversation about the relevant fact, or inviting enquiry about it. But plausibly, it makes both active and passive deception *prima facie* impermissible. I recognise that this is a roughly sketched argument in favour of a more expansive conception of how D's deception operates on V's reasons for and against sex. It does not purport to be a fully worked out thesis.

4.3 Rationale 2: Breach of Trust—Domination and Self-Betrayal

> Impersonation involves a greater breach of trust compared to other illegitimate means of securing sex.

The reason there is a greater breach of trust is because D *intends* for V to consent to sex rather than wanting her to refuse consent. Therefore, D co-opts V against herself, making her a participant in her own violation.[21] She is tricked, not overpowered. As in *R v McNally*,[22] she may feel 'stupid' for believing and trusting D, for not being more careful. Crucially, it is a breach of trust that engenders in V a sense of *self-betrayal*. This is likely to result in feelings of self-blame, guilt, and indeed shame.

[20] I appreciate that the question of sexual orientation is complex. How we resolve this issue would seem to depend on the prior determination of the question of sex/gender. Then again, where someone is bisexual or pansexual, or gender fluid, it may not be possible to definitively say what the nature of the sex was. The point, however, is that V has the right to choose, according to her own desires, beliefs, and commitments.

[21] It is for this reason that some scholars equate rape with torture. See Aswad (1995); Blatt (1991); Gaer (2011); McGlynn (2009); Sussman (2005); MacKinnon (2006). My point is narrower: that rape by deception is analogous to torture in this specific sense of deep self-betrayal.

[22] [2013] EWCA Crim 1051.

For those who observe the multiplicity of rape's harms, such feelings matter.[23] Indeed, there may be a parallel with the structure of torture here. For example, MacKinnon understands rape as torture on the basis of sex.[24] She goes on to implicate the state in such 'abuses,' through its acquiescence or participation.[25] This matters because state acquiescence is needed to bring this otherwise private violation within the international legal definition of torture.[26] Thus, in adopting a broader reading of the impersonation provision, the state would escape this difficulty.

I also note Bergoffen's observation on the use of rape as a weapon of war.[27] She suggests that in focusing on the physical pain of torture, we neglect the significance of the *confession* and the consequent humiliation this inflicts on the victim.[28] The confession, crucially, endorses 'the truth of the torturer's world,'[29] as the victim 'is now named as an accomplice to a world where their values are despised.'[30] This reference to values is important because it is through the body that we instantiate our values. As she puts it, as subjects we 'bring meaning and value to the world' through our embodiment.[31] Such meaning making powers are an aspect of human dignity.[32] Bodily abuse destroys such powers, and in so doing, inflicts a dignity violation.

If we apply this argument to rape, the parallels are there. First, in consenting to sex under induced false beliefs, V, in effect, *confesses*. I think this word implies two things: capitulation and complicity. This is because V is not only tricked, but caused to exercise her agency in a manner that strips her of her power.[33] This is the sense in which it is like a confession. By consenting (invalidly) to what is done to her, she becomes a participant in her own violation. She endorses D's fiction. Secondly, I suggest that in all rape, the victim is dominated.[34] To explicate my understanding of this, I draw on Sartre's concept of our existing as a 'being-for-others.'[35] This concept of being-for-others describes our sense of shame when we realise that we are being observed. This is because we are aware of being judged by others. All rape involves D's judgment, and arguably also that of society. It involves D imposing his truth of who V is—that she is an object to be used—which V can merely *try* to oppose. As Bergoffen notes, such opposition confirms D's power.[36] But rape is not merely

[23]For example, Lacey (1998); Cahill (2001).

[24]MacKinnon (2006).

[25]Ibid, p. 23.

[26]See McGlynn (2008) on this point.

[27]Bergoffen (2019).

[28]Ibid, p. 313.

[29]Ibid, p. 315.

[30]Ibid, p. 315.

[31]Ibid, p. 312.

[32]Ibid, p. 312.

[33]More will be said about power and agency in what follows.

[34]Friedman (2004) for an account linking male domination and diminishment of female autonomy.

[35]Sartre (1956).

[36]Bergoffen (2009), p. 316.

being-for-others, for V has no real opportunity to attempt opposition. Thus, D's truth cannot but prevail, and it is in this sense that V is dominated. I suggest that we can capture this sense of domination with the idea of being-*only*-for-others. This contrasts with ordinary sexual interaction, in which each person manages (or seeks to do so) their respective 'being-for-others' in a reciprocal (if not mutual or egalitarian) interaction. This is why agency (and not merely autonomy) is so important. V must have the chance to exercise her power to make meaning and to oppose the other's judgment.[37]

The ability to oppose the other's judgment is even more important in a pornographised culture.[38] Madden Dempsey and Herring's thesis on the negative social meaning that sexual penetration ordinarily carries is relevant here.[39] They argue that sexual penetration is a prima facie wrong that requires justification due to its negative social meaning. Accordingly, whereas I suggested above that ordinary consensual sex involves both parties managing their beingness-for-others, a more accurate description is perhaps needed. I suggest that whenever sexual penetration is marked by negative social meaning, despite its being consensual, there is a moral asymmetry problem. Thus, while the woman who is sexually penetrated exists as a being-for-others, the man as sexual penetrator escapes (purportedly) his beingness-for-others. This is because, while the woman who is sexually penetrated may oppose the judgment of the man as sexual penetrator, this does not mean that she can oppose the social judgment inherent in the meaning of the act. This meaning involves the 'devaluation of women *qua* women and a disrespecting of women's humanity.'[40] By contrast, the man as sexual penetrator gains power through the meaning of the act, which favours him and elevates him in status.[41] In Bergoffen's terms, he escapes 'the vulnerability and bodied visibility inherent in the intersubjective human condition.'[42] There is a parallel here with Herring's distinction between strong and weak consent.[43] He explains that consent in a strong sense reflects a higher standard in which the person must be maximally free, aware, and empowered to choose in their best interests; whereas consent in a weak sense is more permissive, in that it may be exercised under non-ideal conditions.[44] Indeed, in ideal circumstances, in which consensual sex occurs without negative social meaning,[45] we might describe

[37] My account of being-*only*-for-others seems to overlap with the concept of objectification and the idea, developed by Wallace (2019), of symmetrical and asymmetrical communication. Further insights may be gleaned from Pineau's (1989) argument for communicative sexuality. More is said about the significance of meaning and judgment in Chap. 10—Concluding Remarks.

[38] I am grateful to Professor Herring for pointing to this wider link.

[39] Madden Dempsey and Herring (2007).

[40] Ibid, p. 486.

[41] Ibid, p. 486.

[42] Bergoffen (2019), p. 27.

[43] Herring (2021), in which he emphasises that consent is a scalar concept, p. 55.

[44] Ibid, p. 55.

[45] We might call this ideal consent to distinguish it from strong consent.

both parties as beings-for-each-other. In sum, the fact that rape involves being-only-for-others, as I have suggested, does not mean that consensual sex is morally unproblematic.

Now, while all rape involves being-*only*-for-others—an inability to oppose D's judgment—I suggest that in rape by deception, V exists as an *unaware*-being-*only*-for-others. While she believes that she can oppose D's judgment if she so chooses, she labours under the false belief that D's judgment is other than it is. Other things equal, it seems better to be aware of one's mistreatment than to be unaware. This is traceable to two ideas: the intrinsic value of knowing, of apprehending reality; and the opportunity to protect oneself that comes with awareness. Certainly, to be unaware has its benefits. Where one does not contemporaneously experience one's violation, it may be easier to distance oneself from it, psychologically and emotionally. But it is otherwise worse to be ignorant of the fact not only that one is dominated, but also that one has played a role in one's own domination. Moreover, V suffers what we might call 'epistemic alienation,' in which her subjective experience is at odds with objective fact. Upon discovery of D's deceit, she will realise that she existed as being-*only*-for-others and not as being-for-others. Thus, her exercise of agency was a sham. This is likely to be disempowering, disconcerting, indeed, humiliating.[46] Consent is supposed to protect V's right to sexual autonomy. Here, instead, it becomes a tool for D to use against her. Consequently, V's exercise of negative autonomy is protected, but her exercise of positive autonomy is fundamentally circumscribed. She can always say 'no'—but she says 'yes' at her peril. Thus, whether she suffers rape comes to depend on the good will of D—just as the torture victim is at the mercy of the torturer.

In sum, deception as to identity reduces V to existing as an *unaware*-being-*only*-for-others. It involves a special breach of trust that entails a sense of self-betrayal. V suffers epistemic alienation due to her ignorance of the fact that she was a being-*only*-for-others, and her agency was a sham. Are there any good reasons to suppose that qualitative identity deception does not share this structure?

4.3.1 Qualitative Identity

Does special breach of trust justify prohibiting deception as to the type of person one is? Both numerical and qualitative identity deceptions co-opt V against herself. In causing V to consent, they inflict self-betrayal. It might be objected that this is no different from ordinary tactics of seduction and persuasion used to secure consent to sex—although we should not assume from the fact that such tactics are commonplace that they do not cause significant harm to women. Might such tactics co-opt V against herself in the same way, at least whenever she regrets succumbing to such

[46] See Margalit (1996) on humiliation. Also, Hörnle and Kremnitzer (2011). For a critique, Kleinig (2011).

tactics? I do not think so. There is an important distinction between inducing V to act upon reasons which apply to her and inducing in V a false belief that reasons apply to her when they do not. Per Gardner, this is the difference between subjective and objective rationality.[47] Whereas Williams attributes the failure to adequately address the problem of sexual deception, in part, to the difficulty of establishing what should count as legitimate seduction versus illegitimate deception,[48] I suggest that understanding the way in which D's behaviour acts upon V's reasons can help. Looking more closely at such tactics will be instructive.

Tactics of seduction and persuasion may supply V with reasons in different ways. These might include: (1) supplying her with new reasons, (2) strengthening her current reasons, making them more appealing, (3) removing reasons she had against consent, (4) weakening her reasons against consent, making them less appealing, or (5) altering the relative weight of her reasons for or against consent. We might object to some or all of these tactics. For example, it seems wrong to aim to give V *new* reasons rather than responding to reasons she independently has. There seems to be a relevant moral difference between creating reasons that were hitherto absent for V and satisfying V's own reasons. Thus, Alexander and Sherwin state, '[a] successful lie distorts the reasoning process of the person lied to, displacing his will and manipulating his action… The liar thus fails to respect the victim's capacity for reasoned self-governance.'[49] Similarly, Herring points out that tactics such as manipulation indicate D's improper use of consent, which should reflect V's assessment of her wellbeing.[50] For Dougherty, it is to treat someone as a mere means.[51] However, even where D's tactics supply new reasons, V at least exercises her autonomy based on reasons that actually apply to her. That is morally quite different from being induced to act *believing* that she has such reasons when she does not, or vice-versa. While there is not space to develop this idea fully, it can be reduced to a single proposition: that in seeking to persuade or seduce V, D must not *dominate* her. Intuitively, D does not dominate V in responding to V's own reasons. He does not dominate her in seeking to convince her of the relative weight of her reasons. But he surely does dominate her when he creates new reasons or removes existing reasons so as to secure consent.

Moreover, self-betrayal does not stem merely from the fact that V consents to what turns out to be against her interests. This fact does not sufficiently distinguish deception from other illegitimate means. After all, V also consents in cases of coercion and pressure. Indeed, the law draws a distinction between consent and

[47] See Gardner (1996). This distinction underpins the structure of justification, which Gardner frames in terms of the combination of explanatory and guiding reasons.

[48] Williams (2021), p. 101.

[49] Alexander and Sherwin (2003), p. 397.

[50] Herring (2021), p. 56.

[51] Dougherty (2021).

submission.[52] The line between a threat and an offer may not be clear,[53] and some commentators question whether such a distinction should be drawn.[54] But V knows when she is consenting that she is doing so under coercion or pressure; in acting against her immediate interests, she is at least protecting her broader interests. That is more like self-preservation. In exercising her autonomy, she has made herself better off than she would have been (although worse off than she *should* have been). And crucially, she is aware of this fact. By contrast, with deception, V, who is unaware that her consent is mistaken, has made herself worse off by participating in an act to which she did not genuinely consent. In conclusion, then, both types of deception involve a special breach of trust by inducing self-betrayal.

4.4 Rationale 3: Vulnerability and Responsibility

> Impersonation renders V both more vulnerable and less "responsible" for the sexual violation which occurs.

This rationale is closely related to the *relational intimacy rationale* above. The motivating idea here is that consent is a less apt concept in established intimate relationships marked (typically) by familiarity, affection and mutual concern. Insofar as more may be assumed, implied, excused, and tolerated in existing relationships, V is rendered *more* vulnerable.[55] She has her guard down. Although she can rarely, if ever, have epistemic certainty about D, she at least has epistemic confidence in someone she knows personally. One reason for this is that one is, in a sense, 'primed' for intimacy in such relationships. This might help to explain why sex with V when she is asleep is only an evidential and not a conclusive presumption under the 2003 Act. The law accepts the possibility that certain relational cues and sexual preferences do not need to be signalled as they have already been established. There is empirical literature to support this position.[56] This means that V exercises her sexual autonomy without the usual caution. This is quite apart from the more fundamental problem, explained above, that the reasons she thinks she has for having sex with D—reasons having to do with *who* D is—do not, in fact, exist.

Turning now to the notion of responsibility, I want to demonstrate that there is a silent 'shared responsibility' premise in the 2003 Act, such that V is expected to take some responsibility for her vulnerability to sexual violation. Indeed, Williams suggests that the law's failure to deal adequately with sexual deception is partly

[52] *R v Kirk* [2008] EWCA Crim 434.

[53] See Tadros (2016).

[54] Chamallas (1987); Schulhofer (1998).

[55] Of course, in another sense, she is less vulnerable because it takes more to demonstrate wantedness than it does to establish consent.

[56] For example, expectations around consent negotiation may be sensitive to type of sexual partner/relationship. See Humphreys and Brousseau (2010).

due to the victim being blamed for being too trusting.[57] I refer to responsibility in a descriptive rather than normative sense. Thus, I do not endorse this premise as a normative matter.[58] Evidence of this silent premise appears in several places within the 2003 Act. For example, sex with V pursuant to involuntary intoxication comes under an evidential presumption regarding consent,[59] whereas voluntary intoxication is treated under the general definition of consent in s. 74. Similarly, that V is asleep or unconscious when sex occurs is merely an evidential presumption and not a conclusive one.[60]

Furthermore, the silent premise is reflected within legal practice more broadly. Most notably, the Crown Prosecution Service is considering proposed revisions to guidance on deception as to gender.[61] Thus, in assessing whether V was deceived, prosecutors are asked to consider whether there was an opportunity for V to learn the suspect's gender, which V 'wilfully ignored'.[62] Might this amount to a de facto duty of enquiry upon V, such that if she fails to take the necessary steps, then she will not be believed if she claims that D's sex mattered to her? Moreover, might the emphasis on gender within the guidance obscure the salience of biological sex/trans status to the question of consent, in practice? Indeed, assuming the instability of gender as a construct, it is unclear why complainants should be expected to understand or have clarity on this. Plausibly, the same is true of sexuality, as the heterosexual-homosexual binary comes under increasing pressure.[63] These shifting sands reflect the fluid, malleable nature of identity, which aligns with this book's central thesis.

The guidance sets out a further question for prosecutors. This asks whether the complainant was exploring her sexuality at the time of the alleged offence. Two concerns arise here. First, it conflates sexual orientation with trans or gender identity. Though related, these are distinct aspects of a person's identity, such that we should not draw inferences from the victim's sexual orientation to gender or trans identity. Secondly, to the extent that the guidance implies that sexual exploration is evidence of ambivalence about gender or trans identity, this should be avoided as unfounded and, in effect, penalising complainants exploring their sexuality, while protecting those not doing so.

There is further evidence of this idea of shared responsibility in the case law. The 'passive-active deception' distinction is, arguably, one example. Passive deception requires non-disclosure of a fact in breach of a duty to disclose, whereas active

[57] Williams (2021), p. 101.

[58] For the contrary view, see Duncan (2007).

[59] Section 75(f), Sexual Offences Act 2003.

[60] Section 75(d), Sexual Offences Act 2003.

[61] Deception as to Gender: proposed revision to CPS legal guidance on Rape and Serious Sexual Offences (RASSO), Chapter 6 – Consent, 26 September 2022. Deception as to Gender: proposed revision to CPS legal guidance on Rape and Serious Sexual Offences (RASSO), Chapter 6 - Consent | The Crown Prosecution Service

[62] Ibid.

[63] Nicholson (2015).

deception requires a positive representation by words or conduct (a lie).[64] However, *R v Lawrance*[65] makes clear that it is the 'so closely connected' test that is determinative. Thus, while it is D's responsibility to tell the truth about matters sufficiently closely connected to the act, it is V's responsibility to satisfy herself about D's veracity in matters not sufficiently closely connected to the act. Of course, where D chooses to lie, this leaves V unprotected in law.[66] Thus, the current law protects V against defendants who are willing to mislead her (through non-disclosure) but not lie to her.

4.4.1 Qualitative Identity

Does D's pretending to be a different kind of person also render V more vulnerable and/or less responsible? In considering whether the vulnerability-responsibility rationale carries over, there are two questions. First, is the nature of the deception such that V has her guard down? Second, are there precautions that V should have taken? It seems reasonable to suppose that the answer to these questions will be fact specific in the case of qualitative identity deception. But let's test this. Let us imagine that D has deceived V about their marital status. This occurred in *Papadimitropoulos v The Queen*,[67] where D induced a false belief in V that they were married, which fact V had made a condition of sexual activity. This meant that V thought she was having sex with someone who was her husband, not merely a boyfriend. Although this is not numerical identity deception, it is analogous in the sense that D-as-husband is the person with whom V is "primed" for intimacy. The question is, who is the person for whom there are reasons *for V* to have sex? It is the person who is related to her in a specific way. Because D and V are in the kind of relationship—in this case, marital—that gives them reasons to have sex with each other (beyond general reasons to have sex),[68] this renders V vulnerable. More precisely, it renders her vulnerable to giving consent.

---

[64] Gibson (2020), p. 87.

[65] *Lawrance* (n 19).

[66] It seems that the guidance relating to trans-identifying defendants will depart from this rule. By requiring Vs to make enquiry about trans status, this suggests that the purported deception is insufficiently connected to the act. Whereas ordinarily, this means that D's have no duty to tell the truth, as in *Lawrance*, the guidance suggests that there is a duty to tell the truth when asked. This seems to restore the active-passive deception distinction, thereby undermining *Lawrance*. Presumably this is because there is uncertainty about the subject-matter of the deception (i.e., whether it is biological sex, gender history, gender status, or trans status). An unexplored possibility is that the subject-matter has to do with the person's anatomy/genitalia. There is, moreover, the deeper question of whether, depending on the subject-matter, it is even right to speak into terms of deception. Quite possibly, a compromise is being struck considering epistemic uncertainty and the need to balance competing interests.

[67] [1957] HCA 74; 98 CLR 249.

[68] There is lively debate on whether there are general reasons *not* to have sex. See, for example: Madden Dempsey and Herring (2007); Wall (2015); Greasley (2021).

But what about deceptions that do not leverage relational intimacy, such as those relating to race, religion, single status, wealth, career, political affiliation, and so on? At first blush, it seems obvious to conclude that V is less vulnerable and more responsible because she should be on notice around those she knows less well, and because she is not "primed" for intimacy.[69] While it is unreasonable to expect V to second-guess whether the person she agrees to have sex with is someone else, it seems entirely reasonable to expect her to exercise caution about someone's traits and attributes. In respect of the former, we don't expect V to enquire into something that is atypical. In respect of the latter, the opposite is true. But on closer inspection, this is too quick, for two reasons.

First, the idea that V is responsible for uncovering D's deception as to such attributes as just mentioned, turns out to be entirely hollow. The reality is that her caution will not protect her. As *Lawrance* makes clear, D is free to lie about 'peripheral' matters. This is made possible by the common law's distinction between fraud in factum vs in the inducement. As a result, if one of these matters is of crucial importance for V, the only way she can protect herself is to refuse to believe anyone and to decline all sex. If, instead, she chooses to (*foolishly*) proceed with sex, she must rely on the good will of D in being honest. This makes her radically vulnerable. It also shows that the very practice of sex can only be sustained through V's trust. This places a heavy burden on V, as it does all women. To then claim that she is responsible for whatever befalls her simply lacks credibility.[70] In sum, even though the rationale carries over here, we have reason to question the moral value of this vulnerability-responsibility standard.

Secondly, let us unpack the notion of being 'primed' for intimacy, which I introduced earlier. As suggested, this reduces to the more basic idea that the nature of the relationship provides V with reasons (in addition to any general reasons we might think there are to have sex) (or removes reasons against) to have sex with the particular person, D, which makes V vulnerable to giving consent. D's impersonation allows him to step into this relationship and benefit from these reasons. What is the source of those reasons? The source is the emotional-relational capital that has been cultivated within the relationship, as well as the personal qualities of the individual D is impersonating. With qualitative impersonation, there may be no emotional-relational capital for D to leverage, in which case it is only the personal qualities doing the work.

---

[69] It is worth noting that we do not expect this of V in a fraud case. There, D cannot escape liability on the basis that V was gullible or his lie trivial. See Herring (2021), p. 57.

[70] Assuming she has made enquiry with D.

4.5 Conclusion

In making the case for the equivalence of numerical and qualitative identity deception, I have explored whether there is a rationale, or rationales, common to both types of deception. It was shown that all three rationales carry over. Although the third rationale is less persuasive, this is a function of its being weakly persuasive even in the case of numerical identity deception. This conclusion as to overlapping rationales bolsters the book's main thesis.

Reports

Deception as to Gender: proposed revision to CPS legal guidance on Rape and Serious Sexual Offences (RASSO), Chap. 6 – Consent, 26 September 2022. Deception as to Gender: proposed revision to CPS legal guidance on Rape and Serious Sexual Offences (RASSO), Chap. 6 - Consent | The Crown Prosecution Service

Reforming the relationship between sexual consent, deception and mistake. Criminal Law Reform Now Network. Consultation, December 2021. media_1027_clrnn3-deception-consultation-paper.pdf

Cases

Kaitamaki v The Queen [1985] AC 147

R v Kirk [2008] EWCA Crim 434

R v Lawrance [2020] EWCA Crim 971, [2020] 2 Cr App R 29

R v McNally [2013] EWCA Crim 1051

Papadimitropoulos v The Queen [1957] HCA 74; 98 CLR 249

Fagan v Metropolitan Police Commissioner [1968] EWHC 1 (QB), [1969] 1 QB 439

R (Monica) v DPP [2018] EWHC 3508 (Admin), [2019] QB 1019

R v Miller [1983] 2 AC 161, [1983] 1 All ER 978, [1983] 2 WLR 539, (1983) 77 Cr App R 17 (HL)

Legislation

Criminal Damage Act 1971

Sexual Offences Act 2003, s. 76(2)(b)

Webpage

Nicholson R (2015) 'I'm a bisexual homoromantic': why young brits are rejecting old labels. 'I'm a bisexual homoromantic': why young Brits are rejecting old labels | Sexuality | The Guardian

References

Alexander L, Sherwin E (2003) Deception in morality and law. Law Philos 22:393–450
Ashworth A (1989) The scope of criminal liability for omissions. Law Q Rev 105(July):424–459
Aswad EM (1995) Torture by means of rape. Geo Law J 84:1913–1943
Bergoffen D (2009) Exploiting the dignity of the vulnerable body: rape as a weapon of war. Philos Pap 38(3):307–325
Bergoffen D (2019) The genocidal politics of rape, shame, and disgust. In: Danielsson SK (ed) War and sexual violence. Brill, Schöningh, pp 15–34
Blatt D (1991) Recognizing rape as a method of torture. NYU Rev Law Soc Change 19:821–865
Cahill AJ (2001) Rethinking rape. Cornell University Press
Chamallas M (1987) Consent, equality, and the legal control of sexual conduct. S Cal Law Rev 61: 777–862
Dougherty T (2021) Deception and consent. In: Schaber P, Muller A (eds) Routledge handbook of the ethics of consent. Routledge
Duncan M (2007) Sex crimes and sexual miscues: The need for a clearer line between forcible rape and nonconsensual sex. Wake For Law Rev 42:1087–1130
Feinberg J (1990) Harmless wrongdoing: the moral limits of the criminal law, vol 4. Oxford University Press, Oxford
Friedman M (2004) Autonomy and male dominance. Soundings: an Interdisciplinary Journal 87(1/2):175–200
Gaer FD (2011) Rape as a form of torture: the experience of the Committee against Torture. CUNY Law Rev 15:293–308
Gardner J (1996) Justifications and reasons. Harm Culpability 103:125
Gibson M (2020) Deceptive sexual relations: a theory of criminal liability. Oxf J Leg Stud 40(1): 82–109
Greasley K (2021) Sex, reasons, pro tanto wronging, and the structure of rape liability. Crim Law Philos 15:159–179
Herring J (2005) Mistaken sex. Crim Law Rev 2005:511–524
Herring J (2021) Why mistakes negate consent. In: Reforming the relationship between sexual consent, deception and mistake. Criminal Law Reform Now Network. Consultation, December. media_1027_clrnn3-deception-consultation-paper.pdf, pp 52–58
Herring J (2022) Criminal law: Text, Cases, and Materials, 10th edn. Oxford University Press, Oxford
Hörnle T, Kremnitzer M (2011) Human dignity as a protected interest in criminal law. Isr Law Rev 44(1–2):143–167
Humphreys TP, Brousseau MM (2010) The sexual consent scale–revised: development, reliability, and preliminary validity. J Sex Res 47(5):420–428
Kleinig J (2011) Humiliation, degradation, and moral capacity: a response to Hörnle and Kremnitzer. Isr Law Rev 44(1–2):169–183
Lacey N (1998) Unspeakable subjects: feminist essays in legal and social theory. Hart Publishing
MacKinnon C (2006) Are women human? And other international dialogues. Harvard University Press, Cambridge

Madden Dempsey M, Herring J (2007) Why sexual penetration requires justification. Oxf J Leg Stud 27(3):467–491
Margalit A (1996) The decent society. Harvard University Press, Cambridge
Mayer R (2007) What's wrong with exploitation? J Appl Philos 24(2):137–150
McGlynn C (2008) Rape as 'torture'? Catharine MacKinnon and questions of feminist strategy. Fem Leg Stud 16:71–85
McGlynn C (2009) Rape, torture and the European convention on human rights. Int Comp Law Q 58(3):565–595
Pineau L (1989) Date rape: a feminist analysis. Law Philos 8(2):217–243
Sartre JP (1956) Being and nothingness, trans. Barnes HE. Washington Square Press, New York
Schulhofer S (1998) Unwanted sex: the culture of intimidation and the failure of law. Harvard University Press, Cambridge
Sussman D (2005) What's wrong with torture? Philos Public Aff 33(1):1–33
Tadros V (2016) Coercion and consent. In: Wrongs and crimes. Oxford University Press, Oxford
Wall J (2015) Sexual offences and general reasons not to have sex. Oxf J Leg Stud 35(4):777–798
Wallace K (2019) The network self: relation, process, and personal identity. Routledge
Williams R (2021) Economic and sexual autonomy. In: Reforming the relationship between sexual consent, deception and mistake. Criminal Law Reform Now Network. Consultation, December 2021. media_1027_clrnn3-deception-consultation-paper.pdf, pp 98–105

Part II
Towards a New Approach

Chapter 5
Identity Formation, Persistence and Change

5.1 Introduction

This chapter surveys the literature (theoretical, philosophical, and empirical) on the concept of identity in its personal, social, and relational dimensions. This review of the literature provides a strong rationale for the thesis. It engages with self and identity theory within the larger branch of sociological study to comprehensively anchor the discussion to follow in Part III. A psychological-plus account is endorsed, which is further developed in Chap. 6.

5.2 Identity in Social Theory

Self and identity theory is a major branch of sociological study. The central and highly valuable proposition of identity theory is that the self is not an atomistic psychological entity, but rather, a multifaceted and organised social construct that is deeply embedded in society. Identities, or 'role identities', are the multiple components of self, formed through social interaction within a specific social structure.[1] Such interaction provides self-meaning for identities which are reflexive,[2] in turn influencing social behaviour. Accordingly, identity is 'the pivotal concept linking social structure with individual action.'[3] In contrast, social identity theory is 'a social psychological theory of intergroup relations, group processes, and the social self.'[4] Its central proposition is that a social category provides a self-definition for the individual that is part of his or her self-concept, in which there exist numerous and

[1] Hogg et al. (1995).

[2] Burke and Reitzes (1981).

[3] Ibid, p. 257.

[4] Hogg et al. (1995), p. 259.

R. Farah, *Rereading Identity Deception in the UK Sexual Offences Act 2003*,
SpringerBriefs in Law, https://doi.org/10.1007/978-3-031-44475-3_5

distinct category memberships varying in their overall importance. Self-definition derives from the wider social attributes attaching to membership of a group. This understanding of identity as both stable and dynamic and changing is an important theoretical assumption underpinning this book's thesis.

5.3 Identity in the Philosophical and Theoretical Literature

Our understanding of identity is complex, multifarious, and evolving. As the literature illustrates, we have multiple criteria or concepts for identity.[5] Approaches to defining the concept of personal identity are thus richly diverse. Most theories focus on the 'reidentification' question. This asks what makes X, a person, at one time numerically identical to Y at another time.[6] Theories roughly divide into reductionism and non-reductionism. In Parfit's terms, these are 'complex' and 'simple' views, respectively.[7] Reductionist theories allow that facts about identity can be analysed via more particular facts—whether about brains, bodies, or something else.[8] On this view, persons can be reduced to 'aggregates of person stages that are bound together, into persons'[9] in virtue of some property that they share. Per the complex view, strong continuity of certain properties is constitutive of someone being the same person across time. Psychological, biological, and anthropological accounts are predominant in the literature, and each can be shown to have merit. Non-reductionist theories argue that we cannot reduce identity to a continuity relation, such as psychological or biological.[10] Per the simple view, strong continuity is merely evidence of being the same person. Schechtman argues that reductionist theories cannot account for her four features of personal existence: survival, moral responsibility, self-interested concern, and compensation.[11] One reason for this is that she rejects the idea that personal identity could be a matter of degree, although some proponents of the simple view allow for this possibility.[12] For other theorists, identity is simply not analysable as a concept.[13]

[5]Tobia (2015), p. 6.

[6]Schechtman (2018).

[7]Parfit (1973).

[8]Olson (2021).

[9]Schroer and Schroer (2014), p. 447.

[10]Proponents of non-reductionism include Reid and Hamilton (1863), Butler (1874); Chisholm (2014); Swinburne (1973).

[11]Schechtman (2018).

[12]See Swinburne (2012) for a useful discussion.

[13]Madell (2015), p. 11.

Neo-Lockean (psychological) accounts of personal identity abound,[14] of which Parfit's psychological continuity account is the most familiar.[15] It is 'neo-Lockean' in that it develops Locke's original account of identity persistence, which identified memories, or self-consciousness, as the relevant continuity relation. Concerns motivating later accounts include the need to account for our everyday moral thinking, respect for the intrinsicality of moral status and the moral necessity of agency,[16] the problem of generous ontology,[17] and the need to reflect our fundamental desire for our own (non-derivative) future existence (i.e., not merely Parfitian survivors).[18] No single account emerges unscathed from sustained critique. Still, the psychological account is the 'favorite candidate' for a criterion.[19] And given what I take to be the necessity of psychology to personal identity, I make use of the Parfitian account in the first stages of the thesis to help illuminate the issues.

5.3.1 The Psychological Criterion

The psychological criterion consists in 'overlapping chains of strong psychological connectedness, itself consisting in significant numbers of direct psychological connections like memories, intentions, beliefs/goals/desires, and similarity of character'.[20] Accordingly, a person at one time is identical to a person at another time if and only if there is psychological continuity between them. On this account, personal identity can be lost where there is a significant change in personality, values, preferences and long-term life plans.[21] Therefore, we might see a person who misrepresents his personality, values, preferences, and so on, as analogous to presenting a numerically distinct person. For example, a person who undergoes a religious conversion would arguably be fundamentally different, adopting new values, desires and goals. Christian terminology of being "born again" has echoes of this new identity. Indeed, such a person might see their old identity as, though bearing some resemblance, wholly alien to the person they are now. Because facts about identity over time just consist in these more particular facts, personal identity is not what matters in survival. Rather, psychological continuity / connectedness ('Relation R'), with the right kind of cause, may be just as good. Moreover, *per*

[14] For example, Lewis (1986); Olson (2003); Shoemaker and Swinburne (1984).

[15] For other accounts, see Lewis (1983); Perry (1972); Nozick (1983); Noonan (2019); Unger (1990).

[16] Noonan (2022).

[17] Johnston (2016); Olson (2010).

[18] See Shoemaker and Swinburne (1984), p. 119.

[19] Noggle (1998), p. 803.

[20] Parfit (1984), p. 207.

[21] Shoemaker (1970), p. 269; see also Perry (1972), p. 463.

Parfit, such continuity and connectedness admit of degree, unlike identity, which is a one-one relation.[22]

Alongside Lockean persons, we might also talk about selves. These are the 'temporal parts of a person,'[23] which are subjects of psychological states. We might call them 'subpersons',[24] or 'personites.'[25] While Parfit points out that talk of selves is not to be taken too literally,[26] there is some value in the sexual offences context. This is because what matters to V is, arguably, not who the person ('D') is as a unity, but his particular presentation in the moment of sexual negotiation. As Schroer and Schroer put it, 'the object of some of our emotions may not be another person timelessly considered, but another person during a period in this person's life'.[27] Indeed, this reference to emotions is not insignificant. Lacey argues that rape law neglects the affective (and corporeal) aspects of the offence.[28] The emotional dynamic between V and D is a part of V's subjective evaluation and decision-making. A relevant theoretical underpinning here is Affect Control Theory, one of three approaches to emotions in social theory. Combining cognitive social psychology with identity theory, it explicates the importance of shared meaning for identity. More importantly for our purposes, it concerns how people feel about changes to their own identities and those of others.[29] To the extent that emotions confirm meanings and identities,[30] the emotional bases of the self are relevant.

5.4 Identity in the Empirical Literature

Theorists observe a myopic focus on numerical identity at the expense of qualitative identity. This is understandable given the implications of a loss of numerical identity.[31] Equally, it is important in law if we are to ensure legal certainty. But it fails to track our deepest concerns about personal identity, both as a matter of prudential and moral concern. Accordingly, there is increasing interest in transcending the limits of the focus on numerical identity. Alongside the failure to engage with qualitative identity as a measure of personal identity, commentators have noted the dichotomous treatment of the numerical-qualitative identity

---

[22] Parfit (1971). For a contrary view, see Lewis (1983).

[23] Schroer and Schroer (2014), p. 445.

[24] Olson (2010).

[25] Johnston (2016, 2017).

[26] Parfit (1984), p. 306.

[27] Ibid, p. 305.

[28] Lacey (1998).

[29] Smith-Lovin (1990).

[30] Barnes (2013), p. 222.

[31] Lyreskog (2021).

distinction.[32] Some elide the distinction between identity and similarity,[33] or challenge it directly.[34] Others maintain the division, and instead posit similarity and psychological connection as two further aspects of personal identity.[35]

Some commentators have argued that these studies conflate personal identity (numerical identity) and similarity (qualitative, or biographical, identity), with participants using concepts in equivocal or confused ways.[36] However, a more recent study by Everett et al.[37] has challenged previous findings. Approaching the issue as a practical matter from the perspective of moral duties, this study sought to determine whether similarity or identity was salient in participants' judgments. The study both confirmed the 'moral self effect' (discussed below) and suggested that intuitions were, at least partially, tracking personal identity and not mere similarity.[38] Furthermore, we must recall that theorists have challenged the distinction itself.[39] For example, it has been argued that a sharp division between similarity and identity is untenable.[40] Indeed, Everett et al. make the important observation that Parfit's psychological criterion, which includes attitudes, beliefs and preferences, has elements of both.[41]

Even if some intuitions track similarity rather than identity, it is considered important to note people's ordinary judgments about identity. In demonstrating that qualitative identity is of moral and practical concern, the literature thus provides a compelling rationale for this book's thesis, which mounts a sustained challenge to sharp division between numerical and qualitative identity.

5.4.1 The 'Moral Self Effect'

Several empirical studies from within the psychological experimental literature have observed the 'moral self-effect' in which changes in moral (and social) traits affect judgments about identity persistence to a greater extent than do other psychological traits.[42] While the moral self effect has been criticised due to its reliance on everyday intuitions, others argue that certain intuitions are 'robust' and that more scholarly

[32] Olson (2008).
[33] Starmans (2022).
[34] Chen and Urminsky (2022).
[35] Tobia (2022).
[36] Starmans and Bloom (2018). Also, Berniūnas and Dranseika (2016).
[37] Everett et al. (2020).
[38] Ibid, pp. 924–925.
[39] Cf. Starmans (2022) who argues that identity and similarity are validly distinguished.
[40] See also Chen and Urminsky (2022).
[41] Everett et al. (2020).
[42] For example, Newman et al. (2014); Strohminger and Nichols (2014).

attention should be given to morality.[43] Indeed, Tobia contends that without moral change, we are not talking about numerical identity change at all.[44] Experimental philosophers have addressed the more precise question of the *direction* of moral change, with negative moral change perceived as more identity-affecting. This may be because moral deterioration signals greater separation from what we perceive to be our ideal, or true moral selves.[45] Indeed, the self is commonly assumed to be 'authentic' and thus morally good.[46] Therefore, knowledge of others' true selves is linked to perceptions of moral goodness.[47]

Moreover, there is an interpersonal dimension, as findings suggest that the type of relationship affects identity attributions. Thus, in the context of friendship, identity disruption was greatest in the case of negative moral change, and vice-versa for hostile relationships.[48] The social psychological literature highlights a difference between two relationship types: communal and exchange.[49] As Clark et al. explain, romantic partners fall within communal relationships, which are marked (normatively) by care and attentiveness to the other, whereas casual acquaintances are exchange relationships.[50] Based on this distinction, we may expect parties to sex to relate to each other as romantic partners or quasi-friends. If so, we would have reason to consider the kind of moral change that might be instantiated in deceptive sex. However, this will not always be true. In anonymous sexual encounters and similar casual interactions where there is little-to-no mutual concern, the opposite inference would be appropriate. Nevertheless, the important point is that our understanding of identity seems to be influenced by the nature and quality of our relationships. [See Strohminger 2018].

New concepts have been proposed to reflect the nuance in ordinary judgments about identity. These include: 'dual character' concept,[51] 'true self',[52] 'transformative experience,[53] and self-continuity.'[54] The concept of self-continuity is closely related to Parfit's idea of partially overlapping selves. Chen and Urminsky posit this concept as a third kind of identity alongside numerical and qualitative, arguing that it better explains the concern we have for our future selves and the role that identities play in our subjective judgments and everyday decision-making.[55] Sexual

[43] Everett et al. (2022).

[44] Tobia (2022).

[45] Christy et al. (2016).

[46] Aquino and Reed II (2002); Strohminger and Nichols (2014); Stanley and De Brigard (2019).

[47] Christy et al. (2017).

[48] Everett et al. (2022)

[49] Clark and Mills (1979); Fiske (1992).

[50] Clark et al. (2020).

[51] Knobe (2022).

[52] For example, Schlegel et al. (2016); Rivera et al. (2019); Strohminger et al. (2017); Christy et al. (2017).

[53] Bloom and Paul (2022).

[54] Tobia (2022).

[55] Chen and Urminsky (2022), pp. 72–73.

negotiation is one such situation where people rely on their subjective judgments about others, such that we should pay attention to how people think about their own identity and the role of identity change in decision-making.

Notwithstanding that the reliability of the intuitions elicited in these experiments is subject to scholarly debate,[56] this literature indicates that we may have 'multiple criteria or concepts of identity.'[57] Such conflicting intuitions may indicate 'folk pluralism,' such that there may be no 'canonical conception'.[58] In law, such pluralism has merit. As Tobin explains, 'Insofar as identity is a necessary or sufficient criterion of blame, responsibility, or ownership, pluralism may be practical.'[59] Indeed, psychological,[60] biological,[61] narrative,[62] and anthropological[63] criteria have all found support. Thus, we might take a differentiated approach, utilising a psychological criterion for punishment, and a biological criterion for other purposes, such as property rights. Accordingly, this book proposes a psychological-plus approach, which incorporates a socio-relational understanding of identity, is appropriate for the sexual offences context.

5.5 Two Questions

Personal identity theory addresses the reidentification question, which tracks persons between points in time. The debate centres on the criterion of personal identity. Some theorists argue that no single relation constitutes continuation of the person. Thus, Schechtman has proposed a 'cluster property model' of what she calls 'person lives.'[64] This model accepts that biological, psychological, and social components are all identity constituting. This is the 'more basic relation', as she puts it. In a similar vein, for Chen and Urminsky, the self-concept should be understood in terms of interrelationship. As they explain, the self-concept comprises not only our memories, personality traits, and morals, but also one's 'beliefs about the causal *relationships* between these features' [emphasis added].[65] Wallace, too, conceives of

[56] Tobia (2022); Chen and Urminsky (2022).

[57] Tobia (2022), p. 5.

[58] Sider (2001).

[59] Tobia (2022), p. 5.

[60] Blok et al. (2005); Strohminger and Nichols (2014); Tobia (2015); Molouki and Bartels (2017); Weaver and Turri (2018).

[61] Nichols and Bruno (2010).

[62] Taylor (1992); Schechtman (2018).

[63] Newman et al. (2014) and Strohminger and Nichols (2014); more recently, Strohminger and Nichols (2014); Prinz and Nichols (2016); Chen and Bartels (2016); Strohminger et al. (2017); Christy et al. (2017).

[64] Schechtman (2018).

[65] Chen and Urminsky (2022), p. 78.

the self (or person) as a cumulative network of interrelated traits, such that numerical identity depends on continuity of an undefined cluster of traits.[66] This book's thesis aligns with this richer understanding of the person.

There is a second question: that of *characterisation*. Schechtman criticises the reidentification approach, particularly when it takes the form of the traditional psychological criterion and its time-slice view of the person.[67] As she argues most persuasively, this neglects what is most interesting and important about persons and fails to provide a rationale for our future concern.[68] Accordingly, she highlights *characterisation*: 'the set of characteristics that make a person who she is.'[69] Alongside character traits, this includes actions, experiences and values.[70] This is the kind of identity involved in an 'identity crisis.'[71] An important aspect of her account is that she endorses identity as a matter of degree. Thus, there are more and less central aspects of a person's psychology, such that some features 'play a more central role than others and are more expressive of who she is.'[72] This relates to the idea of one's sense of self—who am I really? It reflects the importance we attach to the continuity of our *characteristics*. Indeed, there is an argument for claiming that the essence of deception as to qualitative identity is that D misrepresents his *self-concept*; and it is this self-concept that V relies on when agreeing to sex. Nevertheless, Parfit's account is equally able to account for degrees of change through the idea of *strong* connectedness,[73] although he would not call this identity *per se*.

5.6 Two Accounts

5.6.1 Narrative Self-Constitution

Various theorists endorse a narrative view of personal identity.[74] Schechtman advances a stronger narrative *self-constitution* view. Narratives, she explains, are 'the lens through which we filter our experience and plans for action.'[75] In so doing,

[66] Wallace (2019), p. 666.

[67] Schechtman (2018).

[68] Ibid, p. 52.

[69] Ibid, pp. 75–76.

[70] Ibid.

[71] Ibid, p. 74.

[72] Ibid, p. 77.

[73] Parfit does not think his account entails the 'Extreme View.' This is the idea that if strict identity is impossible, then the special concern we have for our future selves must be irrational. Thus, I would have no more reason to feel special concern for my future self than I do for present others with whom I am qualitatively similar.

[74] For example, Taylor (1992); Schechtman (2018).

[75] Schechtman (2018), p. 113.

she argues that we *create* our identities. Objections to Schechtman's account have been adequately highlighted elsewhere.[76] For example, Christman argues persuasively that narrativity is not necessary for counting as a single person. Instead, 'interpretive reflection' is sufficient.[77] The important point is that narrative identity presupposes numerical identity, given that we must persist as persons to be self-narrators.[78] For this reason, psychological continuity is indispensable, and the central question concerns what else we think matters.

5.6.2 A Psychology-Plus Criterion

There has been no shortage of proposals for what else matters. Thus, we might combine psychological continuity with the narrative view to provide a unified account of what it means to be a human person.[79] After all, to be able to identify psychologically with successive selves matters. Agency also seems to matter.[80] Perhaps also self-creation.[81] Unger's physicalist view adds a 'core psychology' condition.[82] In an account that pre-dated her stronger self-constitution view, Schechtman argued that only the psychological view could explain the deep importance of identity.[83] Her alternative psychological account addressed our status as temporally extended selves, with pasts and futures that are part of our psychological lives. Her account posits an individual's self-conception as a human being as 'a general organizing feature of psychological life,' such that it enables us to extend our consciousness over time, actually affecting the quality of that consciousness.

A phenomenological approach to psychological continuity has also been proposed.[84] Instead of locating persistence in stand-alone traits, this approach looks for phenomenal or experiential continuity of the right sort. It thereby addresses 'that particular part of mentality that has a what-it's-likeness.'[85] Similarly, McMahan proposes an embodied mind account, locating persistence in the basic capacity for (phenomenal) consciousness.[86] Lyreskog modifies this account to rectify its neglect of important qualitative aspects of identity in relation to dementia.[87] His revised

---

[76] Noggle (1999); Williams (1998); Strawson (2004).
[77] Christman (2004).
[78] Assuming an autobiographical account.
[79] DeGrazia (2005).
[80] Korsgaard (1989).
[81] DeGrazia (2005).
[82] Unger (1990), p. 109.
[83] Schechtman (2018).
[84] Duncan (2020).
[85] Ibid, p. 2031.
[86] McMahan (2002).
[87] Lyreskog (2021).

account can be summarised as follows: 'We are essentially embodied minds. The criteria for personal identity persistence over time are (a) physical and minimal functional continuity of the brain, and (b) a retention of personality, values, and relationships of a higher order.'[88] Notwithstanding that there is a question as to the practical possibility of such features of the self being supported by minimal consciousness, Lyreskog's contribution reflects a clear pattern, in which theorists combine quantitative and qualitative aspects to better explain personal identity.

Greenwood's version of the psychological criterion locates personal identity in the maintenance of fundamental beliefs, principles, and commitments; by means of which we explain the intentional behaviour of persons.[89] This links to the significance of norm internalisation to individual behaviour. For example, a strong personal commitment to a group may lead to endorse normative beliefs, which direct how one thinks one ought to think or behave.[90] When these 'basic psychological principles' change, persons behave differently; they become different persons.[91] In other words, whenever behaviour is explicable by reference to a different set of integrated fundamental beliefs, principles, and commitments, there has been a change in personal identity. Kahan et al.'s notion of 'cultural cognition' lends support to Greenwood's thesis.[92] This refers to the way in which both perception and reasoning (key drivers of action) are influenced by cultural values and commitments. In respect of the degree of change required, Greenwood suggests that more than minor differences are needed; a different set of such features must emerge. Thus, we attribute personal identity to someone, which Greenwood also terms 'singular personhood', given the set of integrated fundamental beliefs, principles, and commitments that explain their intentional behaviour.

The important aspect of Greenwood's account is that it links *who* a person is with *what* the person is through the causal explanatory role these psychological features play in a person's agency. In our context, this would mean that because D deceives V about his beliefs, principles, and commitments in order to secure V's consent to sex, he commits deception as to identity. Thus, in *R (Monica) v DPP*, D misrepresented himself as having strong environmental beliefs and a related ideological commitment to activism. However, Greenwood's account does not seem able to support convictions in deception cases not involving ideological or political commitments. On the other hand, we could think about the idea of commitments in a more abstract way. For example, a commitment to being honest in sexual matters would count. There is some overlap here with Benson's concept of 'the unthinkable'—that we define the boundaries of our identities through what we are unwilling to do.[93] This, therefore, provides another approach to the question of identity change. However, it

[88] Ibid.

[89] Greenwood (1994).

[90] Duckitt (1989), p. 70.

[91] Greenwood (1994), p. 29.

[92] Kahan et al. (2012).

[93] Benson (2003).

reduces to the proposition that we constitute ourselves through our choices. While this is uncontroversial as a proposition, it is of little practical use to claim that an unlawful deception as to identity is any deception chosen by D. Moreover, it implies a supremely broad sexual offences law that would have few supporters.

Greenwood's 'set of commitments' account finds support elsewhere. In general terms, it fits within the emerging significance of moral (and social) traits to personal identity. Thus, Hitlin posits values as the *core* of personal identity.[94] For Drummond, a change in a person's underlying commitments entails identity change.[95] Archer argues that our identities are constituted (not merely evidenced) by our commitments.[96] And Lay, observing the importance of moral features, proposes the idea of 'moral connectedness' as a gloss on Parfit's psychological criterion.[97] This latter account dovetails with the empirical literature in which the 'moral self-effect' was observed.

In a similar vein, Taylor is critical of the abstract, neutral approach to defining the person or self.[98] Instead of the 'punctual' or 'neutral' self whose only constitutive property is self-awareness,[99] the self, for Taylor, is 'something which can exist only in a space of moral issues.'[100] Any account must reflect what matters to us: 'But what has been left out is precisely the *mattering*. The self is defined in neutral terms, outside of any essential framework of questions.'[101] Therefore, our sense of the person must be defined by reference to the relevant constitutive concerns. Other scholars share a similar concern.[102] For example, Naffine observes the role of power in how the moral and legal character of the person is defined. As she explains, 'These posited artificial legal subjects are poorly defined. They lack the basic attributes of real individuals, such as a sex, a race, an age or even a social context. They are universalised rather than particularised.'[103] This suggests the importance of developing a richer concept of the person, understood in terms that include his or her history and context.

---

[94] Hitlin (2003, 2011).

[95] Drummond (2021).

[96] Archer (2015a, b).

[97] Lay (2019).

[98] Ibid, p. 49.

[99] Ibid, p. 49.

[100] Taylor (1992), p. 49.

[101] Ibid, p. 49.

[102] See Norrie (2014), p. 26; Lacey et al. (2010), p. 95.

[103] Naffine (2019).

5.7 Conclusion

This chapter has shown that the concept of personal identity is dynamic, complex, and indeterminate. We have multiple criteria and concepts, with no consensus on persistence conditions. Theorists typically argue about what else persons are beyond self-awareness. If there is an overlapping consensus, it is twofold. First, that mental properties are at least a necessary condition for personal identity, whatever else we think important. Second, that our concept of identity should reflect what matters to us. This may include values, core psychology, social traits, moral orientation, and so on. Accordingly, I endorse a psychology-plus account, while remaining agnostic about the precise properties that might be necessary. What is missing from the discussion so far is an account of the relevance of social and other relationships, as well as the interrelationships among these different elements. In the next chapter, I will explore this question.

Cases

R (Monica) v Director of Public Prosecutions (2018) EWHC 3508 (Admin)

References

Aquino K, Reed A II (2002) The self-importance of moral identity. J Pers Soc Psychol 83(6):1423

Archer MS (2015a) Socialization as relational reflexivity. In: Donati P, Archer M (eds) The Relational Subject. Cambridge University Press, pp 123–154

Archer MS (2015b) The relational subject and the person: self, agent, and actor. In: Donati P, Archer M (eds) The relational subject. Cambridge University Press, pp 85–122

Barnes B (2013) The elements of social theory. Routledge

Benson C (2003) The unthinkable boundaries of self: the role of negative emotional boundaries in the formation maintenance and transformation of identities. In: Harre R, Moghaddam FM (eds) The self and others: positioning individuals in personal, political, and social contexts. Praegger/ Greenwood

Berniūnas R, Dranseika V (2016) Folk concepts of person and identity: a response to Nichols and Bruno. Philos Psychol 29(1):96–122

Blok S, Newman G, Rips LJ (2005) Individuals and their concepts. In: W-k Ahn W-K, Goldstone RL, Love BC, Markman AB, Wolff P (eds) Categorization inside and outside the laboratory: essays in honor of Douglas L. Medin. American Psychological Association, pp 127–149. https://doi.org/10.1037/11156-008

Bloom P, Paul LA (2022) Uncomfortable decisions. In: Tobia K (ed) Experimental philosophy of identity and the self, 1st edn. Bloomsbury Academic, London, p 157

Burke PJ, Reitzes DC (1981) The link between identity and role performance. Soc Psychol Q 44: 83–92

Butler J (1874) The analogy of religion, natural and revealed, to the constitution and course of nature, Of personal identity. Of the nature of virtue, vol 1. Clarendon Press

Chen S, Bartels DM (2016) Beliefs about the causal structure of the self-concept determine which changes disrupt personal identity. Psychol Sci 27(10):1398–1406
Chen S, Urminsky O (2022) What's left of me? In: Tobia K (ed) Experimental philosophy of identity and the self, 1st edn. Bloomsbury Academic, London
Chisholm R (2014) Person and object: a metaphysical study, vol 17. Routledge
Christman J (2004) Narrative unity as a condition of personhood. Metaphilosophy 35(5):695–713
Christy AG, Seto E, Schlegel RJ, Vess M, Hicks JA (2016) Straying from the righteous path and from ourselves: the interplay between perceptions of morality and self-knowledge. Personal Soc Psychol Bull 42(11):1538–1550
Christy AG, Kim J, Vess M, Schlegel RJ, Hicks JA (2017) The reciprocal relationship between perceptions of moral goodness and knowledge of others' true selves. Soc Psychol Personal Sci 8(8):910–917
Clark MS, Mills J (1979) Interpersonal attraction in exchange and communal relationships. J Pers Soc Psychol 37(1):12
Clark MS, Earp BD, Crockett MJ (2020) Who are "we" and why are we cooperating? Insights from social psychology. Behav Brain Sci 43(e66):21–23
DeGrazia D (2005) Human persons: narrative identity and self-creation, Human Identity and Bioethics, pp 77–114
Drummond JJ (2021) Self-identity and personal identity. Phenomenol Cogn Sci 20(2):235–247
Duckitt J (1989) Authoritarianism and group identification: a new view of an old construct. Polit Psychol 10(1):63–84
Duncan M (2020) A new argument for the phenomenal approach to personal persistence. Philos Stud 177:2031–2049
Everett J, Skorburg JA, Savulescu J (2020) The moral self and moral duties. Philos Psychol 33(7): 924–925
Everett J, Skorburg JA, Livingstone J (2022) Me, my (moral) self, and I. https://kar.kent.ac.uk/83701/1/Everett%20et%20al%20%282021%29%20Moral%20Self.pdf
Fiske AP (1992) The four elementary forms of sociality: framework for a unified theory of social relations. Psychol Rev 99(4):689
Greenwood JD (1994) A sense of identity: prolegomena to a social theory of personal identity. J Theory Soc Behav 24(1):25–46
Hitlin S (2003) Values as the core of personal identity: drawing links between two theories of self. Soc Psychol Q 66:118–137
Hitlin S (2011) Values, personal identity, and the moral self. In: Schwartz SJ, Luyckx K, Vignoles VL (eds) Handbook of identity theory and research, Vol 2. Springer, New York, pp 515–529
Hogg MA, Terry DJ, White KM (1995) A tale of two theories: a critical comparison of identity theory with social identity theory. Soc Psychol Q 58:255–269
Johnston M (2016) Personites, maximality and ontological trash. Philos Perspect 30:198–228
Johnston M (2017) The personite problem: should practical reason be tabled? Noûs 51(3):617–644
Kahan DM, Hoffman DA, Braman D, Evans D, and Rachlinski JJ (2012) They saw a protest: cognitive illiberalism and the speech conduct distinction. Stanford Law Rev 64:851–906
Knobe J (2022) Personal identity and dual character concepts. In: Tobia K (ed) Experimental philosophy of identity and the self, 1st edn. Bloomsbury Academic, London, p 49
Korsgaard C (1989) Personal identity and the unity of agency: a Kantian response to Parfit. Philos Public Aff 18:103–131
Lacey N (1998) Unspeakable subjects: feminist essays in legal and social theory. Hart Publishing
Lacey N, Wells C, Quick O (2010) Reconstructing criminal law: text and materials, 4th edn. Cambridge University Press, Cambridge
Lay C (2019) Why Parfit's psychological criterion does not work as a personal identity theory (and how it could)
Lewis D (1983) Survival and identity. In: Philosophical papers, vol I, online edn. Oxford Academic, New York. https://doi.org/10.1093/0195032047.003.0005
Lewis D (1986) On the plurality of worlds. Blackwell, Oxford

Lyreskog DM (2021) Withering minds: towards a unified embodied mind theory of personal identity for understanding dementia. J Med Ethics:1–8. https://doi.org/10.1136/medethics-2021-107381
Madell G (2015) The essence of the self: in defense of the simple view of personal identity. Routledge, p 11
McMahan J (2002) The ethics of killing: problems at the margins of life. New York, Oxford University Press
Molouki S, Bartels DM (2017) Personal change and the continuity of the self. Cogn Psychol 93:1–17
Naffine N (2019) Criminal law and the man problem. Bloomsbury Publishing
Newman GE, Bloom P, Knobe J (2014) Value judgments and the true self. Personal Soc Psychol Bull 40(2):203–216
Nichols S, Bruno M (2010) Intuitions about personal identity: an empirical study. Philos Psychol 23(3):293–312
Noggle R (1998) Marya Schechtman, The constitution of selves: the constitution of selves. Ethics 108(4):802–805
Noggle R (1999) Integrity, the self, and desire-based accounts of the good. Philos Stud 96(3): 303–331
Noonan HW (2019) Personal identity. Routledge
Noonan HW (2022) Personal identity and morality. In: Tobia K (ed) Experimental philosophy of identity and the self, 1st edn. London, Bloomsbury Academic, pp 87–97
Norrie A (2014) Crime, reason and history: A critical introduction to criminal law, 3rd edn. Cambridge University Press, Cambridge
Nozick R (1983) Philosophical explanations. Harvard University Press
Olson ET (2003) An argument for animalism. In: Martin R, Barresi J (eds) Personal identity. Blackwell, Oxford, pp 318–334
Olson ET (2008) Personal identity. In: Stich SP, Warfield TA (eds) The Blackwell guide to philosophy of mind. John Wiley & Sons, pp 352–368
Olson ET (2010) Ethics and the generous ontology. Theor Med Bioeth 31:259–270
Olson ET (2021) Personal identity. In: The Stanford encyclopedia of philosophy, Spring edn https://plato.stanford.edu/archives/spr2021/entries/identity-personal/
Parfit D (1971) Personal identity. Philos Rev 80:3–27. https://doi.org/10.2307/2184309
Parfit D (1973) Later selves and moral principles. In: Montefiore A (ed) Philosophy and personal relations, 1st edn. Routledge
Parfit D (1984) Reasons and persons. Clarendon Press, Oxford
Perry J (1972) Can the self divide? J Philos 69(16):463
Prinz JJ, Nichols S (2016) Diachronic identity and the moral self. In: Kiverstein J (ed) The Routledge handbook of philosophy of the social mind, 1st edn. Routledge, pp 465–480
Reid T, Hamilton W (1863) The works, vol 1. Edinburgh, Maclachlan and Stewart
Rivera GN, Christy AG, Kim J, Vess M, Hicks JA, Schlegel RJ (2019) Understanding the relationship between perceived authenticity and well-being. Rev Gen Psychol 23(1):113–126
Schechtman M (2018) The constitution of selves. Cornell University Press, Ithaca
Schlegel RJ, Hicks JA, Christy AG (2016) The eudaimonics of the true self. In: Vitterso J (ed) Handbook of eudaimonic well-being. Springer, Cham, pp 205–213
Schroer JW, Schroer R (2014) Getting the story right: a reductionist narrative account of personal identity. Philos Stud 171(3):445–469
Shoemaker S (1970) Persons and their past. Am Philos Q 7(4):269–285
Shoemaker S, Swinburne RG (1984) Personal identity. Blackwell, Oxford
Sider T (2001) Criteria of personal identity and the limits of conceptual analysis. Philos Perspect 15: 189–209
Smith-Lovin L (1990) Emotion as the confirmation and disconfirmation of identity: an affect control model. In: Kemper TD (ed) Research Agendas in the Sociology of Emotions. State University of New York Press, pp 238–270

Stanley ML, De Brigard F (2019) Moral memories and the belief in the good self. Curr Dir Psychol Sci 28(4):387–391
Starmans C (2022) Identity crisis. In: Tobia K (ed) Experimental philosophy of identity and the self, 1st edn. London, Bloomsbury Academic
Starmans C, Bloom P (2018) Nothing personal: what psychologists get wrong about identity. Trends Cogn Sci 22(7):566–568
Strawson G (2004) Against narrativity. Ratio 17(4):428–452
Strohminger N (2018) Identity is essentially moral. Atlas of Moral Psychology, pp 141–148
Strohminger N, Nichols S (2014) The essential moral self. Cognition 131(1):159–171
Strohminger N, Knobe J, Newman G (2017) The true self: a psychological concept distinct from the self. Perspect Psychol Sci 12(4):551–560
Swinburne RG (1973) Personal identity. In: Proceedings of the Aristotelian Society, vol 74. Aristotelian Society, Wiley, pp 231–247
Swinburne RG (2012) How to determine which is the true theory of personal identity. In: Gasser G, Stefan M (eds) Personal identity – complex or simple? Cambridge University Press, pp 105–122
Taylor C (1992) Sources of the self: the making of the modern identity. Cambridge University Press
Tobia KP (2015) Personal identity and the Phineas Gage effect. Analysis 75(3):396–405
Tobia KP (ed) (2022) Experimental philosophy of identity and the self, 1st edn. Bloomsbury Publishing, London
Unger P (1990) Identity, consciousness and value. Oxford University Press
Wallace K (2019) The network self: relation, process, and personal identity. Routledge
Weaver S, Turri J (2018) Personal identity and persisting as many. Oxf Stud Exp Philos 2:213–242
Williams C (1998) The constitution of selves. Philos Rev 107(4):641–644

Chapter 6
The Social-Relational Self

6.1 Introduction

Identity has social, relational, and personal dimensions.[1] Theorists drawing attention to the social and relational nature of the self argue that considering one dimension of identity in isolation provides only a partial picture of what is most important about identity. This prompts the question: Should we look at the concept of identity through a broader lens for the purpose of the impersonation provision? I think there are three main advantages of positing a richer conception of the person. First, to reflect selves as they *actually* are.[2] Second, to rethink what matters about deception as to identity. I hope to achieve this through an alternative analytical-theoretical framework. And third, to justify expanding the scope of the impersonation provision. Accordingly, this chapter endorses a socio-relational conception of the person, or self. Its aim is to support the argument in Chap. 9 that seemingly small changes in traits can translate into substantial changes at the level of the self.

In this endeavour, I draw on the work of Kathleen Wallace[3] and Charles Taylor[4] to suggest a theoretical framework for rethinking the impersonation provision. From Wallace's work, I borrow the idea that traits are dynamically interrelated. While endorsing her dynamic and expansive account of traits, I diverge from Wallace in terms of what this implies about identity persistence. From Taylor's work, I borrow the idea that the self is dialogical. However, before engaging with the work of Wallace and Taylor, I must first provide an overview of social and relational theories of the self. This is not a comprehensive review. The aim is simply to foreground, and

[1] Lopes and Teresa (2012).

[2] This question animates the work of, for example, Schechtman (2018); Gendler (2002), pp. 34–35; Wallace (2019), p. 26.

[3] Wallace (2019).

[4] Taylor (1994).

R. Farah, *Rereading Identity Deception in the UK Sexual Offences Act 2003*,
SpringerBriefs in Law, https://doi.org/10.1007/978-3-031-44475-3_6

provide a rationale, for the approach later in the book in respect of the relationship between identity and traits/attributes.

6.2 The Self in Social Theory

The conception of the self in terms of social relationships and interactions ties to several aspects of social theory. First, it implicates social constructionism. According to Haslanger's prominent account, we are each socially constructed in the sense that who we are as individuals is largely determined by what has been attributed to us, including our self-attributions.[5] Such attributions reflect not objective reality, but how things are related to us.[6] This conveys the important point that who we are is not entirely in our own gift. Yet, this does not imply that we are wholly determined by others. Rather, to be constructed is to have the features that qualify as belonging to a certain kind.[7] Secondly, it implicates interactionist sociology, which addresses the emergence of the self, the self-concept, and the presentation of the self.[8] Goffman considered society as a series of encounters among individuals who are precisely *not* autonomous, pre-constituted, and fixed in their nature or properties.[9] Indeed, Barnes notes the suggestion in some iterations of interactionist theory that people are continually constituted and reconstituted in interaction.[10]

Finally, Benson proposes the concept of 'unthinkable boundaries' and 'the unthinkable' as a measure of what kind of person one is.[11] The unthinkable is the boundary between being one sort of person and not another. 'As she explains, 'Self's integrity or oneness, its unity or type, is a function of the kinds of boundary that, it is assumed, "contain" the system that is self.'[12] Thus, alongside bodily boundaries which are identity defining, so too are psychological boundaries. Though less tangible, these are highly significant for selfhood and identity. As Benson puts it, 'Simply put, I am what I can and will do, but also, of neglected significance, what I cannot do and will resist doing.'[13] This suggests that we self-constitute ourselves not only through what we do, but also through what we decide not to do.

---

[5] Haslanger (2012).

[6] Ibid., p. 109.

[7] Ibid., p. 123.

[8] Ritzer and Smart (2000), p. 220.

[9] Barnes (2013), p. 70.

[10] Ibid.

[11] Benson (2003).

[12] Ibid.

[13] Ibid, p. 64.

6.3 The Relational, Social Self

The ideal of the 'autonomous man' reflects an individualistic view of the self. This is the dominant view in law. However, there is an anti-individualist turn in the theoretical and philosophical literature, steered by feminist scholarship. The notion of the self as an atomistic, self-sufficient entity separated and independent from others has thus been eclipsed by new accounts of the self. This chapter endorses such reconceptualisations, positing the self as a 'subject-in-relation'[14]—a dynamic, relational, interdependent entity that is constituted by social and other relations.[15] Alongside relationships with others, one's position in society and thus structures of society are crucial to identity formation.[16] As will be shown, the idea that identity is constituted through relationships and social structures is well grounded in the literature.[17] Accordingly, when we think about identity change, we must consider relationships, social and moral traits, and social organisation and processes.

6.3.1 *The Relational Self*

This notion is tied to the idea that persons are constituted by their relations with others. This is not simply that relationships are a central component of our identities; it is the stronger assertion that the self is formed and developed *only* through its interpersonal, societal, and institutional relations.[18] Thus, the self is, *itself*, relational. Various theorists endorse this view. Baier introduces the notion of 'second persons' to explain the relational self. Thus, early development of the self requires interaction with caregivers and others to bring persons into being.[19] As Mackenzie notes, '... [t]o be a person is to be a temporally extended embodied subject whose identity is constituted in and through one's lived bodily engagement with the world and with others.'[20] This links social theory with phenomenology, in which the body is accorded a constitutive role in consciousness.[21] For Brison, both selfhood and distinctive selves depend on relationships. Thus, she writes, 'I am a self by virtue of my relations to others—and I am the particular self I am by virtue of my relations

---

[14] Donati and Archer (2015), p. 15.

[15] This leaves open whether persons are *fully* constituted by social relations. For Donati and Archer (2015), persons are only partly so constituted.

[16] Ricoeur (2015).

[17] For example, Honneth (1995); Mead (1934).

[18] Brison (2017). See also relational autonomy theorists, such as Mackenzie and Stoljar (2000); Meyers (1989); Nedelsky (2011).

[19] Baier (1985).

[20] Mackenzie (2009), p. 119. See also Mackenzie (2014).

[21] Ritzer and Smart (2000), p. 239.

to particular persons.'[22] And Calhoun emphasises the meaning and motivational force we derive from important relationships.[23] Both our character and self-understanding are fixed by means of our relationships.[24]

It is important to note the complex and dynamic nature of a person's composition of traits or attributes. Brison points out that living simultaneously in different cultural and linguistic communities has implications for who we are.'[25] Thus, whether or not an attribute is present or absent may depend on the particular context the individual happens to be in. Maria Lugones represents this idea through her notion of different 'worlds'. This is the idea that because we can inhabit different worlds at once, it is intelligible to describe ourselves as both having and not having an attribute of some sort.[26] This is an important point for our purposes. It indicates the multiplicity of a person's inner world, in which many different configurations of attributes are possible. They may be multiple, changing, and, indeed, conflicting, at any given moment. As I will discuss later in this chapter, Wallace's network theory illuminates this important reflection.

6.3.2 *The Social Self*

As individuals, we are socially embedded. In classical feminist social theory, the individual is a social actor with embodied subjectivity and a dynamic and multifarious inner life 'marked by agentic subjectivity—by capacities to think and to will, by ethical orientation and by irrepressible desire.'[27] Accordingly, there is a dynamic relationship between self and society in which the individual social actor and social processes are deeply intertwined.'[28] Thus, social life is both inherently relational[29] and processual in nature.[30] 'A "person" or "individual" is thus not a self-contained entity or unit, she or he does not exist 'in themselves', they only exist as elements of sets of relations with other individuals.'[31] Bourdieu, in arguing that we need to think relationally, understands this in terms of 'fields'.[32]

I endorse the view that selves exist in relation to other selves, and that they shape and are shaped through interaction with those other selves. That the self emerges out

[22] Ibid, p. 226.

[23] Calhoun (2008), p. 197.

[24] Herring (2013).

[25] Brison (2022), p. 222.

[26] Lugones (1987), p. 3.

[27] Ritzer and Smart (2000), p. 133.

[28] Ibid, p. 133.

[29] Elias (1991), p. 19.

[30] Elias (1997), p. 371.

[31] Ritzer and Smart (2000), p. 356.

[32] Bourdieu (1990), p. 192.

of social interaction is a key insight of symbolic interactionism.[33] The stronger claim is that selves do not exist *except* in relation to other selves—that we are constituted in and through others.[34] It is not necessary to determine this issue here. The important point is that the fundamentally social nature of the self is theoretically well grounded.

6.4 Towards an Analytical-Theoretical Framework

With the above in mind, I propose a theoretical framework which posits an intersubjective, relational self to articulate a broader range of identity deceptions—those centring on *what kind of person* D claims to be. The central proponent of the 'dialogical self'[35] being Charles Taylor, I use Taylor's work connecting identity to the good[36] to foreground my concluding *Substantial Difference (SD)* thesis. Alongside this, I engage with Kathleen Wallace's *Cumulative Network Theory*,[37] which provides theoretical grounding for the idea that persons (or what she calls 'selves') are highly dynamic, complex systems. Together, I treat these as provide a useful lens through which to understand identity change.

An important question is what the threshold is for identity change. That is, what kind or degree of change should occur, such that we consider someone to be a different person. Such change could inhere in core psychology,[38] values,[39] moral deterioration or improvement,[40] enough overlapping psychological connections,[41] the capacity for basic consciousness,[42] basic consciousness plus other features,[43] loss of one's inner story,[44] or the integrated set of fundamental beliefs, principles, and commitments.[45] While I do not seek to answer this question here, I make some suggestions in Chap. 9. As I argue there, if D *would be* a different person had the subject-matter of his deception been true, the law should treat him as though he *is* that different person and deny him the benefit of his deception. I thus offer a hybrid descriptive-normative account that makes a novel contribution to the debate.

---

[33] Ritzer and Smart (2000), pp. 219–20.
[34] Brison (2022), p. 218; Baier (1985), p. 84.
[35] Taylor (1995).
[36] Taylor (1992).
[37] Wallace (2019).
[38] Unger (1990).
[39] Hitlin (2003).
[40] Tobia (2022); Chen and Urminsky (2022).
[41] Parfit (1984).
[42] McMahan (2002).
[43] Lyreskog (2021).
[44] Schechtman (2018); Taylor (1992).
[45] Greenwood (1994).

6.4.1 *Wallace's Cumulative (Relational) Network*

The concept of a relational or social self has its source in feminist and communitarian theory. It conceives of the person, or self, as constituted by social and other relations. I refer to this understanding of the self as 'social-relational'. The narrative view is an example. Narration is relational, involving how one is constructed socially by others.[46] Some argue that this view tends to fix the identity of the person. Instead, as persons, we change over time, vary in our self-conceptions, and no two identities are the same.[47] Wallace seeks to avoid this problem by positing the self as a network of traits and relations. From Wallace's theory, I take the idea of the persistent yet changeable self. *Contra* Wallace, I propose that a self may *not* survive certain changes and losses of traits.

Wallace conceives of the relational self as an overall system of uniquely interrelated traits and history. As she explains, it is 'a complex of plural constituent relations, that is, a *network* of traits, with synchronic unity, and a *process*, that is, a temporal spread with diachronic unity.'[48] This is her cumulative network model (CNM) of the self, comprising interrelated biological, genetic, physical, social, psychological, linguistic, semantic, and other traits.

The unique contribution of Wallace's thesis is her dynamic and expansive account of traits, which explains the complexity and variability of the system she posits. Traits are qualities or properties but not in the sense of permanence or immanence.[49] Accordingly, in the CNM, traits are not necessary conditions. Instead, they are more like family resemblances.[50] Because all traits are themselves relational, with no hierarchical structure, there is a high degree of variability. Moreover, given the reflexive nature of the self, traits may conflict and require resolution. They are features of, for example, 'personality, interpersonal relationships, personal values, socio-economic position,'[51] and so on. Some traits are defining in terms of their relevance to the self's identity at a given moment. But only some of these defining traits will be persistent and all traits will vary in terms of the strength of their impact on the cumulative whole. Accordingly, Wallace groups strongly relevant clusters of traits into sub-networks or 'hubs'—three of which she identifies as bodily, family, and social role.[52] A further important aspect of her account is that some traits are chosen by the individual, while others are not.[53] Indeed, the individual may be unaware of the existence of certain traits.

---

[46] Brison (2022); Campbell (2003).

[47] Christman (2004), p. 145.

[48] Wallace (2019), p. 8.

[49] Buchler (1990).

[50] Wallace (2019).

[51] Ibid, p. 31.

[52] Ibid.

[53] Ibid, p. 29.

In terms of identity change and persistence, the key claim from Wallace is that the self may persist even through substantial change as long as '*some* cluster of traits' prevails.[54] This is because she hangs the idea of numerical identity on the self as an overall system, comprising interrelated traits and history, which can tolerate substantial change. The *system* of traits must continue. As she puts it, 'it is that self-as-it-is-up-to-now, albeit diminished.'[55] Although Wallace accepts that a system may be destroyed by some 'damage or alteration,'[56] she does not indicate what cluster of traits is necessary for the self to persist.

So, how does this relate to the thesis of this book? I think there are three areas of significance. First, Wallace's theory supports the idea that small changes in traits can engender significant change in respect of the whole. In Meyers' terms, the infinite possible combinations among diverse traits interacting together lends the self an inchoate quality.[57] Indeed, just a single trait interacting with another trait may have profound effects. Secondly, might we treat strongly relevant traits, given their greater importance in the self's identity, as a proxy for substantial change? Certainly, this would offer a metric for distinguishing significant from insignificant deceptions. Thus, we might ask: 'Which trait or traits conditioned D's behaviour in the sexual encounter?' We have good reason to take this approach in the context of sexual relations given the importance of sexuality to self-identity[58] and its 'complex involvement in both physical and affective relations.'[59] Thirdly, if history is a trait, this has implications for the debate around trans-identifying defendants whose gender history is in issue—not to mention other aspects of a person's history. This then raises the question: does my right to know who you are include knowing who you *were*? Less obviously, might it include who you aspire to be? For Wallace, a self is constituted not only by its relations to its past but also by its relations to its future, which includes its possibilities.[60] This is because of the cumulative aspect of the self which projects itself into the future. Importantly, this allows for personal reinvention. Though it is beyond the scope of this project to address such questions, and it raises concerns regarding foreknowledge, agency, and freedom,[61] Wallace's theory is highly relevant to theorists tackling this issue.

---

[54] Wallace (2019), p. 666.

[55] Ibid, p. 665.

[56] Ibid, p. 666.

[57] Meyers (2020), p. 629.

[58] Some may disagree about this. And as I argue in Chap. 10, this has implications for circumstantial pressure cases, including *R v Linekar* 1995] QB 250, [1995] s All ER 230.

[59] Childs (2001), p. 311.

[60] Wallace (2019), p. 195.

[61] For discussion, Hunt (1997).

6.4.2 Taylor's Dialogical Self in Moral Space

Taylor articulates a conception of the dialogical self, in which our communicative interaction with others is a necessary condition for emergence of the self: 'We become full human agents, capable of understanding ourselves, and hence of defining our identity, through our acquisition of language'.[62] Thus, for Taylor, we exist within 'webs of interlocution,'[63] through which we interact with others, forming individual identities and constructing social reality. It is also through language that our agency is shared with others.[64] Hermans and Gieser, in describing the dialogical self as a 'dynamic multiplicity of relatively autonomous 'I-positions,' observe that 'In the interplay between positions and counter-positions the agency of the self comes to its full expression.'[65] In contrast with a Hobbesian account of our basic condition as atomistic, self-interested, and competitive, we become who we are through our relationships with important others.

Some feminist theorists reject the individualised conception of the self, emphasising our dependency relations.[66] Alongside feminists, those in the communitarian tradition address the limitations of the model of the autonomous self.[67] For example, Herring challenges law's self-understanding and its myopic focus on individual rights. He articulates a theory of the relational self that can be of practical use in law, in which relationships and caring responsibilities are framed as a core element of identity.[68] Indeed, the self can only be described in reference to other selves.[69] A crucial concept here is that of recognition. Our relationships are said to involve mutual recognition, which is necessary for identity formation.[70] Honneth's theory of the struggle for recognition is the source of this line of thought. Honneth understands a person's 'relation-to-self' as dependent on processes of mutual recognition which occur during a person's life. Taylor points out that identity is shaped not only through recognition, but also through nonrecognition and misrecognition.[71]

Taylor rejects the defining of self in neutral terms without reference to other selves and questions of concern.[72] We are, he claims, more than mere self-awareness, which is simply not what matters to us.[73] We are centrally motivated by our defining relationships, including our intimate relations, and our search for

---

[62] Taylor (1994), p. 5.

[63] Ibid, pp. 35–36.

[64] Taylor (1994), p. 41.

[65] Hermans and Gieser (2011), p. 660.

[66] For example, Kittay (2009).

[67] For example, MacIntyre (1984, 1988); Sandel (1988); Honneth (1995).

[68] Herring (2020), p. 9.

[69] Ibid, pp. 35–36.

[70] Honneth (1995).

[71] Taylor (1994), p. 25.

[72] Taylor (1992).

[73] Ibid, p. 49.

meaning. His account points to the essential role that other persons play in our identity construction and maintenance. As socially embedded, relational creatures, our interests and life stories overlap with those of other people. On one view, this makes it difficult to imagine one's own welfare and flourishing apart from those with whom we are meaningfully related.[74] As Taylor observes:

> I define who I am by defining where I speak from, in the family tree, in social space, in the geography of social structures and functions, in *my intimate relations* to the ones I love, and also crucially in *the space of moral and spiritual orientation within which my most important defining relations are lived out.*[75]

Here, Taylor situates the self within moral space. As he states, '... our being selves is essentially linked to our sense of the good, and that we achieve selfhood among other selves.'[76] This rejection of neutrality in favour of what is significant for self and others seems an important insight. It is reflected in the emerging attention on moral and social traits in the literature. For Taylor, 'We essentially *are* (i.e., define ourselves at least inter alia by) where we stand on this.'[77] Thus, being connected to the good or to fundamental value is 'essential to being a functional human agent.[78] Taylor seems to put our self-definition in stronger terms than does, for example, Christman. Discussing the social constitution of the self, he writes, 'Interpersonal *connections*, dominant public meanings, one's social location, family history, and so on figure prominently in the full list of components that make up the self.'[79] Accordingly, a relation need not be *intimate-loving* or *most important defining* for it to be self-constituting.

Reflecting on the above, several points arise. First, one is led to ask: If where D stands goes to his self-definition (therefore the question of identity), might this strengthen V's right to know about what is significant to D? This relates to the notion of self-understanding, or self-interpretation. Taylor writes, 'To ask what a person is, in abstraction from his or her self-interpretations, is to ask a fundamentally misguided question, one to which there couldn't in principle be an answer.'[80] This suggests V's right to know about D's self-concept, including his commitments, values, relations, and so on. Secondly, I think we can combine two ideas from Taylor's work—language and space—to generate further insights. We have seen that Taylor appeals to the dialogical nature of identity, conceiving of the self in relation to language and culture. In this, he draws a crucial connection with agency, which he says we share with others through language. My interest in agency here is its connection with intentional action, that is, D's intention to deceive V into sex. Now, we can think of sexual relations as a conversation between V and D. Other

[74] Foster and Herring (2017).

[75] Taylor (1992), p. 35. Emphasis added.

[76] Ibid, p. 51.

[77] Ibid, p. 33. Emphasis added.

[78] Ibid, p. 42.

[79] Christman (2004), p. 104. Emphasis added.

[80] Taylor (1992), p. 21.

interlocutors are undoubtedly involved,[81] such as the wider society which gives the act of sexual penetration its negative social meaning.[82] The self (and subjectivity) cannot be separated from its social constitution and location, including relations of power and the impact of institutions. This undermines the possibility of the autonomous self.

Equally, his spatial metaphor is useful. We can think of sexual relations in terms of a space. To reflexively navigate and control the norms of this relational space requires (borrowing from Taylor's analogy) both a map and knowledge. Both are required for V to understand and critically evaluate this space, setting boundaries where she needs to, and allowing 'incursions'[83] only where these align with her self-identity—like a country might open its borders to those who share its values and close it to those who are hostile to it. Deception operates to deny V the opportunity to assert control over this space, and indeed to determine its boundaries, which threatens the sense she has of herself.[84] For Christman, who endorses a socio-historical conception of the self, the autonomous person is one who is able to understand, manage and integrate (reflexively and coherently) the norms, institutions, practices and relations within one's social location. This is a useful insight for our purposes. It suggests that V's sexual autonomy is not exhausted by her ability to say 'yes' or 'no' to sex. It requires that she be autonomous in relation to this sexual relational space.

Sexual offences law, more fundamentally, in shaping the norms of sexual practice to allow many deceptions, leaves this space greatly circumscribed in relation to V. Consequently, with many of the boundaries V tries to set being denied legal effect, a sexuality or sexual identity is imposed on her that she might not otherwise choose. If she wishes to extend this space, she runs enormous risks. In contrast, D has a vast space within which to practice his own sexuality and self-identity. The law protects this space from the incursions of V who might wish to assert control over the norms of the practice. Thus, in *R v Lawrance*,[85] V sought to extend this space by asserting the right to set a condition on sex that was not reflected in a legal norm. This attempt failed, such that the issue of fertility is excluded from this space.

In sum, this discussion suggests to me that we should take more seriously deception that implicates one's conception of the good where this affects V's ability to understand, critically evaluate and navigate the space of sexual relations. Only this affords her autonomy in relation to the social space that is her body in sexual relations. Accordingly, I propose that significant change or loss to moral traits,

[81] Communitarian theorists, such as MacIntyre (1984, 1988) and Sandel (1988) address this question.

[82] Madden Dempsey and Herring (2007).

[83] I use this word deliberately to invoke the idea of sexual penetration as a pro tanto wrong that requires justification. See Madden Dempsey and Herring (2007). See Chap. 4 for further discussion.

[84] Christman (2009).

[85] [2020] EWCA Crim 971.

which implicate relations with significant others, *can* be identity altering in the relevant respect.

6.4.3 Community and Communities

A further important aspect of both accounts is the importance Taylor and Wallace attach to the notion of community. For Taylor, there are two dimensions of identity definition. The first is our stand on moral and spiritual issues, and the second is our relation to a defining community. His notion of community is distinctly communitarian in the sense of being related to social, political, religious, geographical, and historic communities. He refers to the 'given' communities of birth and history, although people can come to reject these allegiances. For Sandel, too, such community allegiances are identity-defining.[86]

Wallace posits the cumulative network self as a reflexive community of perspectives. This means that it can 'take a perspective' on itself.[87] The idea that one may consist in a plurality of selves or first-person perspectives is not new,[88] and various theorists endorse reflexive communication as a way of conceiving the interaction among different self-perspectives.[89] More interestingly for our purposes, she conceives of community in terms of 'experiential parallelism' that prompts signifying or interpreting activity in relation to 'a common object or condition for mutuality'.[90] While Wallace offers an intrapersonal account of the concept of community, I think it enables us to focus on the interpersonal, social dimension. Thus, we can think of a community of sexual actors sharing a common experience of sexual relations. As Wallace makes clear, signifying/interpreting activity within a community need not be harmonious, the object need not be problematic, and it does not require all members to know or to be communicating with one another. But members must 'share some common perspective or contribute (consciously or not) to a common, overall direction... or experience something in common... that promotes signifying activity.'[91] Similarly, in his account of our dependence on others for our selfhood, Taylor draws on the idea of shared meanings which emerge through conversation. Thus, both self-definition and self-understanding are only achieved 'through my and others' experience of these being objects for us, in some common space.'[92] Unlike Wallace who seems to posit an already existing common object, for Taylor the object

[86]Sandel (1988), p. 179.

[87]Wallace (2019), p. 119.

[88]For example, Mead (1934).

[89]See Mead (1934); Royce (2001); Buchler (1990). This relates to dialogical self theory, which brings Wallace and Taylor's work together neatly.

[90]Wallace (2019), p. 117.

[91]ibid, p. 118.

[92]Ibid, p. 35.

is constituted as common to the parties through their talking about it.[93] But, importantly, both theorists centre communication and interpretation as an essential aspect of the question of identity.

Borrowing from the above, we might think of a more specified community, such as the community of those who are sexually penetrated and those who sexually penetrate. Alternatively, we can posit a community of consent-givers and one of consent-seekers—both communities being part of the larger community of sexual actors. Or a community of sex-sellers and sex-buyers within this larger community. This prompts the question: Might deception as to *community* be a normatively significant kind of deception? Combining Wallace's insights with Taylor's communitarianism may be useful. If such communities are so integral to the self, even if later rejected, this suggests that deception in relation to them has moral relevance.

Wallace adapts this concept of the community as experiential parallelism to the self. Thus, she articulates the variety of different "I-positions" or "I's" from which the self takes a perspective on itself. This perspective can take different forms. It may relate to itself as a whole, or as it was in the past, as it wishes to be in the future, and so on. It may involve broader perspectives, such as political allegiances, or social or economic status. She notes that I-positions may also share a common perspective. This contribution from Wallace is useful for our purposes. I think it allows us to ask several questions. For example, what is the I-position from which the self understands, interprets, and seeks to define its sexual experience? We can think of a case such as *R v Linekar*.[94] Plausibly, I-as-prostitute involves the subordination of sexual desire to the client. Accordingly, I-as-purchaser-of-sex involves the receipt of sexual subordination from the prostitute. What is the I-position that is conditioning D's behaviour in this interaction? For example, I suggest that in *R v B*,[95] D's sexual perversion was the relevant I-position. This conflicted with the I-position appropriate to D's status as V's boyfriend. Thus, an important question concerns what is the I-position that stands in such conflict to a common sexual experience that D will not reveal it? In *R v Jheeta*,[96] this was D's I-position as blackmailer. Finally, is I-as-desirer-of-sex in conflict with I-as-desirer-of-something else? This recalls *R v Devonald*[97] where D's true purpose was humiliation, not sexual gratification. We can interpret such deception as an aspect of identity conceived of in terms of I-positionality. In sum, some or all of these perspectives V potentially has the right to know about, subject to a fully worked out account of how the different I-positions interrelate, their relative salience in the particular context, and how they cause V to be treated. At the very least, asking such questions can help to challenge our thinking about the kinds of deceptions that go to identity.

---

[93] Ibid, p. 35.

[94] [1995] 3 All ER 69 73.

[95] [2013] EWCA Crim 823.

[96] [2007] EWCA Crim 1699.

[97] [2008] EWCA Crim 527.

6.5 A Network of Selves in Moral-Relational Space

We can now think more clearly about when loss (or gain) of traits means that someone is like a different person. Drawing on Wallace's work, I propose three possible grounds: (1) loss or major change to a hub (2) change to a relevant I-position, and (3) loss of a strongly relevant trait. Drawing on Taylor's work, I propose two further grounds: (1) loss or major change to socially or morally salient traits, and (2) loss or major change to an identity-defining relationship, or to a relationship within the space of sexual relations. This discussion foregrounds the argument to follow in Chap. 9, which I present as a Substantial Difference thesis.

Three features of Wallace's conception of traits must be understood. First, because each trait is related to some other traits in different and distinct ways, there is a high level of complexity between traits and sub-networks of traits. Each relation generates a whole web of relations within a given network. This is important for our purposes because it accounts for enormous variability. On Wallace's view, such variability means that numerical identity persists through considerable internal change. The self is a process, the 'cumulative upshot' of all that has gone before.'[98] Indeed, the self's history—'the prior cumulative network of relations'[99]—is another trait. Thus, the self can tolerate loss of traits, changes to traits, diminishment, and even loss of higher, self-reflexive capacities. In a similar vein, Benson defines the self in terms of 'extremely complex, multi-layered processes that are capable of being stabilized as continuities while remaining open to great variation and change.'[100] Related to this is the idea that no single trait is essential to personal identity. Rather, they are more like family resemblances.[101] Secondly, while some traits are chosen or 'self-determined' by the person, others are not. There is disagreement about whether it is intelligible to imagine ourselves being able to reject social identities.[102] For Christman, the social-historical nature of the self means that the self is, to some extent, *held* in the social context that governs its self-definition, along with many of its social relations.[103] Furthermore, the relative weight of our self-defining traits will often be beyond one's control. As Christman puts it, '[W] hich factor among the multiple aspects of our identity becomes prominent may often be pressed upon us by external treatment or social location.'[104] This is important because in Chap. 9 I argue that D may have identities that are socially constructed by others, even those which he personally rejects. Thirdly, Wallace claims that clusters of traits can be organised into 'hubs' or 'sub-networks' of the self as the overarching

[98] Wallace (2019), p. 69.

[99] Ibid, p. 69.

[100] Benson (2003), p. 61.

[101] Similarly, Battersby (2006), pp. 40–41, observes that the self is not identifiable either with a single trait or all taken collectively. Instead, the self both encompasses and transcends them all.

[102] Christman (2009), p. 202.

[103] Ibid, p. 10.

[104] Ibid, p. 202.

network. She identifies three such hubs as bodily, family, and social.[105] This aspect lends support to the *Substantial Difference Argument* presented in Chap. 9, such that a self may be treated as ceasing to exist long before Wallace allows.

6.5.1 Testing the Framework

We can test the utility of this framework by applying it to a hypothetical example involving deception as to a person's religion. As outlined at the beginning of this chapter, it is a principle of social identity theory that a person's characteristics are tied to their membership of (understood as participation in, or identification with,) specific groups. Identity is thus bound to social categories.[106] Religious affiliation, is plausibly, an important social category. Indeed, it has been noted that religious groups are a potent motivational factor in both collective and personal action.[107] Religion is 'often a defining feature of both personal and collective selves.'[108] Indeed, Mayor and Ysseldky report that the 'reciprocal relationship between personal and social aspects of identity... is particularly potent in the case of religious identities, by their potentially all-encompassing nature.'[109] Religion is a community in both Taylor's and Wallace's terms.

Where a person claims a different religion or no religion, this can amount to deception as to a sub-network or hub—or to a community (properly defined). We might treat this as change of the kind, or degree, that justifies treating someone as a different person. By contrast, if a person were to falsely claim they were part of a different faith denomination, this would not be change to a hub; but merely change *within* a hub. However, it would be change to that specific denomination's community within the larger community of religious persons. Similarly, we could imagine someone lying about their wealth. I discuss this in Chap. 9. But essentially, I think the question here is which other traits and networks are implicated in a single trait or traits. A lie about a single trait might implicate a person's class or socio-economic position, for example. Thus, we might compare someone who is unemployed with no savings who claims to be a millionaire with someone who claims to be financially stable when in fact he has significant credit card debt. In this sense, there is overlap between the degree of deception and the idea of change to a sub-network or hub. But they do not strictly track each other.

---

[105] We might propose, in addition, a cultural-linguistic hub, a class hub, and perhaps also an intimate-sexual hub.

[106] Akerlof and Kranton (2000), p. 720.

[107] Mavor and Ysseldyk (2020), p. 191.

[108] Ibid.

[109] Ibid, p. 187.

I suggested that we might ask whether a particular trait was socially or morally salient.[110] However, this is fraught with difficulty. From whose perspective do we judge salience? If that of society, then this hardly improves upon the current legal position. The academic literature reflects disagreement about who decides when a deception is material. For some, this should be judged from the perspective of the victim as a subjective matter. For others, the law should set a standard.[111] The alternative ground I have suggested is loss or significant change to an identity defining relationship. On this point, I derive a different conclusion from Wallace.[112] For example, she discusses the problem of severe dementia and the effect this has on relationships. She is clear that the patient survives even extreme loss of reflexive capacities. She relies on the idea that the patient's relationships remain, which ensures the patient is someone deserving of respect and dignity. But I think this is too quick, for reasons relating both to the dynamic interrelationships of traits and the role others play in our identity formation and maintenance, as I will now explain.

Wallace is surely right that the relationship has not been lost, but it is fundamentally different. It is helpful to refer to Lindemann's theory of 'holding and letting go' within the social practice of personal identities here.[113] Although, for example, the parent-child relationship still exists, there should be a 'letting go' of people in their identities. Per Lindemann, it seems wrong to treat the person who has changed significantly according to stories that no longer apply to her. Certainly, per Wallace's concept of the cumulative self, a person's history is one of their relevant traits. But what about deep personality change or values and behaviours that reflect identity *conflict* or *crisis*? On my view, there has been an important change to the quality of relationship, albeit not necessarily its nature. For relational identity theorists, such relational change entails change at the level of the self.

Admittedly, whether we should venture to say that there has been a role reversal, or the instantiation of new roles, is controversial. To suggest, for example, that the mother has become the child, and the child the mother, relies on contested ideas about caring roles and dynamics. As Herring observes, '[I]t is common and natural for children to care for their parents, and it is only the glorification of adulthood that disguises that reality.'[114] Yet, I think we can say that there has been an important change to the lived-in reality of the relationship even if its formal status remains the same.[115] This seems to be a morally relevant difference, which, per Lindemann, will involve some 'letting go' of certain aspects of the person. To suggest that such aspects remain part of the self, considered cumulatively, neglects the role of others in shaping and maintaining our identities. Certainly, different people will hold and let

---

[110] Per Herring (2005); Also, Dougherty (2013).

[111] Per Gardner (1996).

[112] Wallace (2019).

[113] Lindemann (2014).

[114] Herring (2021), Abstract.

[115] I am grateful to Professor Jonathan Herring for pointing out this distinction.

go differently.[116] This is even more reason to think that the significance of personal change cannot be decisively determined without reference to relationality and relationships of care. In sum, I do not think the cumulative account can accommodate (for all purposes) such kinds of deep relational and/or moral transformation.

6.6 Conclusion

More will be said in the final chapter about how we should assess identity change. This chapter has shown that personal identity is a complex, dynamic, and multi-faceted process that is simultaneously marked by continuity. The importance of one's identity is a foundational assumption of social theory, including sociology and social psychology.[117] For this reason, the discussion was anchored in identity and social identity theory. The chapter endorsed a socio-relational conception of the person, or self. Drawing on the work of Wallace and Taylor, it presents an alternative analytical-theoretical framework through which we should understand identity as it relates to sexual deception. This framework will be applied in Chap. 9, in which the final stage of the equivalence thesis is set out.

Cases

R v Devonald [2008] EWCA Crim 527
R v B [2013] EWCA Crim 823
R v Linekar [1995] 3 All ER 69 73
R v Lawrance [2020] EWCA Crim 971
R v Jheeta [2007] EWCA Crim 1699

References

Akerlof G, Kranton R (2000) Economics and identity. Q J Econ 105(3):715–753
Baier A (1985) Theory and reflective practices. In: Postures of the mind: essays on mind and morals, NED - New edn. University of Minnesota Press, Minneapolis, pp 207–228
Barnes B (2013) The elements of social theory. Routledge
Battersby JL (2006) Narrativity, self, and self-representation. Narrative 14(1):27–44
Benson C (2003) The unthinkable boundaries of self: the role of negative emotional boundaries in the formation maintenance and transformation of identities. In: Harre R, Moghaddam FM (eds)

116 Lindemann (2014).
117 Carr (2021).

The self and others: positioning individuals in personal, political and social contexts. Praegger/ Greenwood
Bourdieu P (1990) In other words. Polity, Cambridge
Brison SJ (2017) Personal identity and relational selves. In: The Routledge companion to feminist philosophy. Routledge, pp 218–230
Brison SJ (2022) Outliving oneself: trauma, memory, and personal identity. In: Feminist philosophy of mind. Oxford University Press, New York
Buchler J (1990) Metaphysics of natural complexes, 2nd edn. SUNY Press
Calhoun C (2008) Losing one's self. In: Atkins K, Mackenzie C (eds) Practical identity and narrative agency. Routledge, New York, pp 193–211
Campbell S (2003) Relational remembering: rethinking the memory wars. Rowman & Littlefield
Carr D (2021) Personal identity is social identity. Phenomenol Cogn Sci 20:341–351
Chen S, Urminsky O (2022) What's left of me? In: Tobia K (ed) Experimental philosophy of identity and the self, 1st edn. London, Bloomsbury Academic
Childs M (2001) Sexual autonomy and law. MLR 64:309
Christman J (2004) Narrative unity as a condition of personhood. Metaphilosophy 35(5):695–713
Christman J (2009) The politics of persons: Individual autonomy and socio-historical selves. Cambridge University Press
Donati P, Archer MS (2015) The relational subject. Cambridge University Press
Dougherty T (2013) Sex, lies, and consent. Ethics 123(4):717–744
Elias N (1991) The society of individuals. Basil Blackwell, Oxford
Elias N (1997) Towards a theory of social processes. Br J Sociol 48(3):355–383
Foster C, Herring J (2017) Identity, personhood and the law. Springer, Cham
Gardner S (1996) Appreciating Olugboja. Leg Stud 16(3):275–297
Gendler TS (2002) Personal identity and thought-experiments. Philos Q 52(206):34–54
Greenwood JD (1994) A sense of identity: prolegomena to a social theory of personal identity. J Theory Soc Behav 24(1):25–46
Haslanger S (2012) Resisting reality: social construction and social critique. Oxford University Press
Hermans HJM, Gieser T (eds) (2011) Handbook of dialogical self theory. Cambridge University Press, New York
Herring J (2005) Mistaken sex. Criminal Law Review, pp 511–524
Herring J (2013) Forging a relational approach: best interests or human rights? Med Law Int 13(1): 32–54
Herring J (2020) Law and the relational self. Cambridge University Press, Cambridge. (Law in context)
Herring J (2021) Children care. In: Clough B, Herring J (eds) Disability, care and family law. Routledge, pp 51–66
Hitlin S (2003) Values as the core of personal identity: Drawing links between two theories of self. Soc Psychol Q 66:118–137
Honneth A (1995) The struggle for recognition—the moral grammar of social conflicts. Polity Press, Cambridge
Hunt D (1997) Two problems with knowing the future. The importance of time: proceedings of the philosophy of time society, 1995–2000, pp 207–223. Dordrecht: Springer Netherlands
Kittay EF (2009) The personal is philosophical is political: a philosopher and mother of a cognitively disabled person sends notes from the battlefield. Metaphilosophy 40(3–4):606–627
Lindemann H (2014) Holding and letting go: the social practice of personal identities. Oxford University Press
Lopes H, Teresa C (2012) The relational dimension of identity – theoretical and empirical exploration. Rev Soc Econ 70(1):81–107
Lugones M (1987) Playfulness, "world"-travelling, and loving perception. Hypatia 2:3–19
Lyreskog DM (2021) Withering minds: towards a unified embodied mind theory of personal identity for understanding dementia. J Med Ethics 49(10):699–706

MacIntyre A (1984) After virtue. A study in moral theory. Duckworth, London
MacIntyre A (1988) Whose justice? Which rationality? Duckworth, London
Mackenzie C (2009) Personal identity, narrative integration and embodiment. In: Campbell S, Meynell L, Sherwin S (eds) Embodiment and agency. The Pennsylvania State University Press, Pennsylvania, pp 100–125
Mackenzie C (2014) Embodied agents, narrative selves. Philos Explor 17(2):154–171
Mackenzie C, Stoljar N (eds) (2000) Relational autonomy: Feminist perspectives on autonomy, agency, and the social self. Oxford University Press, New York
Madden Dempsey M, Herring J (2007) Why sexual penetration requires justification. Oxf J Leg Stud 27(3):467–491
Mavor KI, Ysseldyk R (2020) A social identity approach to religion: religiosity at the nexus of personal and collective self. In: The science of religion, spirituality, and existentialism. Academic Press, pp 187–205
McMahan J (2002) The ethics of killing: problems at the margins of life. Oxford University Press, Oxford
Mead GH (1934) Mind, self and society: from the standpoint of a social behaviorist. University of Chicago Press, Chicago
Meyers DT (1989) Self, society, and personal choice. Columbia University Press
Meyers DT (2020) Reflexive communication and the whole self: Kathleen Wallace's the network self. Metaphilosophy 51(5):628–634
Nedelsky J (2011) Law's relations: a relational theory of self, autonomy, and law. OUP, Oxford
Parfit D (1984) Reasons and persons. Clarendon Press, Oxford
Ricoeur P (2015) Soi-même comme un autre. Média Diffusion
Ritzer G, Smart B (eds) (2000) Handbook of social theory. Sage
Royce J (2001) The problem of Christianity. CUA Press
Sandel M (1988) Liberalism and the limits of justice, 2nd edn. Cambridge University Press, Cambridge
Schechtman M (2018) The Constitution of selves. Cornell University Press
Taylor C (1992) Sources of the self: the making of the modern identity. Harvard University Press, Cambridge
Taylor C (1994) The politics of recognition. In: Gutmann A (ed) Multiculturalism: examining the politics of recognition. Princeton University Press, Princeton
Taylor C (1995) The dialogical self. In: Goodman RF, Fisher WR (eds) Rethinking knowledge: reflections across the disciplines. State University of New York Press, Albany, pp 57–66
Tobia K (ed) (2022) Experimental philosophy of identity and the self, 1st edn. Bloomsbury Academic, London
Unger P (1990) Identity, consciousness and value. Oxford University Press
Wallace K (2019) The network self: relation, process, and personal identity. Routledge

Part III
Equivalence Thesis

Chapter 7
Equivalence Thesis: Stage A

Equivalence Thesis (A): Earlier Self Impersonation
P^1: It is impermissible to engage in two-body numerical impersonation[1]
P^2: Single-body numerical impersonation and two-body numerical impersonation are, other things equal, on a par in terms of permissibility
C^1: Therefore, single-body numerical impersonation is impermissible—let us call this *earlier self impersonation*

7.1 Introduction

This chapter presents the first stage (A) of the Equivalence Thesis in relation to s. 76 (2)(b) (the impersonation provision) of the Sexual Offences Act 2003. It critically analyses the concept of identity in this provision against that employed in this first stage of the thesis. It thus connects the theoretical-philosophical work engaged in thus far with positive law, drawing implications for law and legal practice. The argument proceeds in stages towards the conclusion that the impersonation provision can accommodate past selves as objects of impersonation. I address a major challenge presented by the provision's 'known personally' requirement. I draw upon the best account of second-person epistemology to do so, showing that a past self is relevantly similar to a past (deceased) person.

[1] Although largely asserted, a short justification is offered.

R. Farah, *Rereading Identity Deception in the UK Sexual Offences Act 2003*, SpringerBriefs in Law, https://doi.org/10.1007/978-3-031-44475-3_7

7.2 Two-Body Impersonation

The moral badness of numerical identity deception is uncontroversial, and it is categorically prohibited in law by virtue of s. 76(2)(b) of the 2003 Act. Few would disagree that everyone has the right to choose the person with whom they will have sex. Quite simply, consent to sex with person A is not consent to sex with person B. A plurality of values grounds this right, including sexual integrity, agency, and 'freedom of sexual choice' as the 'primary value of criminalisation'.[2] Without further argument, then, the first premise is established.

7.3 Single-Body Impersonation

Turning to the second premise, a paradigmatic case of numerical impersonation will be called *two-body* impersonation. This type of impersonation involves two metaphysically distinct persons—in separate bodies—one of whom pretends to be the other. This is distinguished from what may be called *single-body* impersonation, which involves impersonation by person-stages or successive selves inhabiting a single body. They will be referred to as P1 and P2, respectively, to reflect the fact that they are *like* different persons.

Assuming Lockean persons, we can posit a defendant who is, at any given, time a person-stage composed of certain 'thoughts, beliefs, desires, and traits of character'.[3] Now imagine a simple case where the defendant (D) is a person, P1, who suffers a severe traumatic brain injury. Because psychological continuity is so severely diminished, P1 has ceased to exist in a Parfitian sense. Clearly, the law would not treat him as though he were now P2. Indeed, the anthropological account would consider pre-injured entity and injured entity to be the same person because they share the same human life. But using Parfit's theory, with the R relation lost, a loss of numerical identity is assumed for argumentative purposes.

Now, taking them to be numerically distinct persons, suppose that P2 were to have sexual intercourse with his girlfriend. Let us assume she is somehow unaware of the profound change he has endured and relates to him as P1. In allowing her to believe that he is still P1, he is impersonating someone *known personally* to the victim (V). This is *single-body impersonation.* Perhaps P2 is not cognitively capable of inducing V's mistake, but he allows her to labour under her false belief. Could this not be, prima facie, a case of rape? At a minimum, it seems to satisfy the general meaning of consent, and is in line with R v *Elbekkay*.[4]

This is not a purely academic question. There are difficult questions around identity and consent in elder care settings where, for example, a woman suffering

[2] Harris (1976), p. 644.

[3] Parfit (1984), p. 207.

[4] [1994] EWCA Crim 1, [1995] Crim LR 163.

from dementia seeks sex with another resident whom she mistakenly thinks is her husband. This unique setting seems to require a nuanced approach that balances a duty of care with dignity, respect, and appropriate autonomy.[5] Indeed, identity might be less morally salient in this context. But in other contexts, assuming the reductionist view of personal identity so described, it is possible for D to feign traits with which he no longer personally identifies, and for this to matter greatly to V.

The critic might point out a morally relevant difference between *single* and *two-body* cases. He might appeal to the fact that in *two-body* case, both persons exist, whereas only one person exists in *single body* case. Person 1 (P1) has ceased to exist and he is now Person 2 (P2) (assuming his cognitive condition is irreversible). Because P1 is "dead", he is necessarily a non-person and, so the reasoning goes, he cannot be impersonated. This certainly raises a valid question: If P1 no longer exists, can he be impersonated in the sense required by the 2003 Act? The next section will argue that allowing once-existing persons to be objects of impersonation is not ruled out by the provision itself.

7.4 Knowing Someone Personally

For the 2003 Act to be coherent, it must be the case that the impersonation provision refers to persons alive or dead. Certainly, there is nothing on the face of it to rule this out. But more than that, if the Act required contemporaneous personhood, this would seem to rule out personal knowing of any kind, given that anything except instantaneous knowing is, logically, a past knowing. And it is an epistemological truth that an object once known, *ceteris paribus*,[6] is always known. Therefore, to place such a narrow reading on the provision when it is otherwise silent appears arbitrary and unmotivated.

It may be objected that the above account conflates propositional knowledge—also termed knowledge by description or knowledge-about—with acquaintance knowledge[7] and thereby fails to account for important features of second-person epistemology (hereafter, 'SPE'). This is the study of how we know other people,[8] which is distinct from other sorts of knowledge claims. On one account of SPE, there is a paradox at the heart of the *single-body* impersonation case just presented. The paradox is this: the fact that P2 is not P1 because P1 no longer exists means that P2's conduct constitutes, prima facie, rape via impersonation. But this same fact seems to mean that P1 cannot be known personally (where personal knowing requires more than propositional knowledge), which means there was no rape by impersonation. The paradox is potentially fatal to this paper's thesis because one needs to be able to

[5] Tarzia et al. (2012), p. 609.

[6] This is subject to the caveat of the object not having undergone extreme change.

[7] Ali and Fumerton (2020).

[8] Talbert (2014), p. 190.

say that a previously existing person-stage or self can be an object of impersonation. In response to this problem, the next section briefly sketches the details of an SPE account in which the paradox is readily apparent. It will be shown that this account is too demanding and that once revised, the paradox disappears.

7.4.1 Resolving a Paradox

There are numerous accounts of the knowledge of persons. These include acquaintance,[9] recognition,[10] and congeniality[11] accounts, and they generally fail to establish necessary or sufficient conditions for personal knowing. Matthew Benton offers a more promising account, centred on interpersonal knowledge.[12] This obtains when two subjects know each other personally, as subjects, from the second-person perspective. It is a 'state of minds meeting',[13] requiring subject-to-subject engagement through enough 'personal encounters of reciprocal causal contact' that is symmetric. Talbert's second-personal account is similar, requiring 'shared worlds, created through shared experiences',[14] although Talbert is concerned with knowing *well*. Both accounts are non-propositional and require that subjects be actually existing.[15]

Matheson[16] provides an alternative, communication account, which is both more and less demanding. He explains that one person knows another 'just in case the first individual knows personal information about the second as a result of the second's having communicated the information specifically to her'.[17] Hence, personal knowing requires 'the agency, or voluntary participation, of those known'.[18] This is the respect in which it is more demanding. Furthermore, the communication from known to knower is intentional, and the information reveals something 'rather intimate'.[19] This latter condition means information that is not readily inferable, rather than something especially secret. Moreover, *pace* Benton and Talbert, this type of knowing is propositional.[20] This is the respect in which it is less demanding. It thereby elides the traditional distinction between acquaintance and propositional

---

[9] Feldman (2003), p. 11.
[10] Craig (1991), p. 147.
[11] Ibid, p. 147.
[12] Benton (2017).
[13] Ibid, p. 813.
[14] Ibid, p. 821.
[15] Ibid, p. 813; Talbert (2014), p. 195.
[16] Matheson (2010).
[17] Ibid, p. 443.
[18] Ibid, p. 347.
[19] Ibid, p. 441.
[20] Zagzebski (2017).

knowledge. It is a matter of having *enough* propositional knowledge gained in the right way—namely, direct testimony. Both Talbert and Matheson have a further non-deception (in important respects), or justified true belief, condition. There is not space to advance a theory of personal knowledge for the sexual context. However, the next section will address the feature that engages the paradox: the requirement for existing persons.

7.4.2 Defining Objects of Impersonation

Benton recognises that there are 'diachronic difficulties' around when interpersonal knowledge 'begins and ends'.[21] In respect of when it ends, the difficulty arises because his symmetry condition entails that interpersonal knowledge is lost for both if lost for one. He argues that 'one must continue to have enough recurring encounters over time in order to keep knowing someone personally'.[22] Thus, it is possible to no longer know someone personally where such encounters either stop or slow. He claims that this explains cases of amnesia and death. In respect of death, the 'factivity' of interpersonal knowledge means that 'there must be a mind there to be known'.[23] Otherwise, interpersonal knowledge is past, with only propositional knowledge of the deceased remaining. Similarly, Talbert argues that knowledge of persons can 'expire'.[24] Therefore, some of the second-person interactions must be 'relatively recent' and probably within the last twenty years. However, because Talbert is concerned with knowing *well* rather than with minimal conditions of knowing, we can reject such an implication.

Even if we were to assume that the provision requires present knowing, the requirement for continual interpersonal knowing once the threshold for interpersonal knowing has been achieved is overly demanding. Because Matheson's account has the advantage that symmetry is not required, the deceased person counterexample is unproblematic. Instead, the argument being proposed is that: because nothing new can be known *personally* about a person once they have died, then, once they have been known, we ought to consider such knowing to be *present* in the sense of persisting. *Pace* Talbert, it does not expire. Thus, to say that a dead person *was* known personally is not necessarily to say that he used to be, but is no longer, personally known. It is to say that when he could be known, he was known. That is, when there was a mind to be known, it was known. And, crucially, it was never re-known. Therefore, it is known as it was and as it always would be.

[21] Benton (2017), 826.

[22] Ibid, p. 826.

[23] Ibid, p. 827.

[24] Talbert (2014), 195.

Lindemann's notion of 'holding and letting go' is helpful here.[25] Lindemann addresses the social practice of forming and maintaining personal identities through our interaction with others. This involves 'holding' people in their identities, while allowing the stories that constitute those identities to evolve along with the person. As she explains,

> To hold someone in her identity is to treat her according to the stories one uses to make sense of who she is. If the identity is to represent accurately the person who bears it, the tissue of stories that constitute it must continue to change as the person grows and changes. Here, 'good holding' is a matter of retaining the stories that still depict the person but letting go of the ones that no longer do.[26]

Lindemann's concern for accurate representation recalls Honneth's concept of recognition, which Taylor develops in his work on identity. Applying the idea of 'good holding' to the present discussion, it could be argued that seeking to 're-know', to know anew, the mind of a person who has died is an example of 'bad holding'. Lindemann allows that identity work may continue after a person has died—whether in terms of the dead holding the living, or the living holding the dead through 'acts of preservative love'.[27] Certainly, it may be common for information about a person to come to light posthumously, and indeed, we may preserve our memory of them in a whole variety of ways. But, *per* Matheson, this would lack voluntary agency and thus would merely be knowledge *that*—in the impoverished sense that Matheson rightly rejects.

7.4.3 Deathbed Letter

A more challenging objection is where someone writes a letter to be read after they have died.[28] One would thereby come to know something new about the person *and* it has the quality of voluntary agency. Perhaps a mother with terminal cancer films a series of video diaries to be played to her young child every year on his or her birthday. This presents a challenge. It seems that on the revised account just outlined, relatives and friends of the now deceased mother would no longer know her personally. This is not simply because their personal knowing has ceased, but because it has continued elsewhere—she has been known *anew*.

This objection can be overcome in two ways. First, it has implausible implications. It suggests that a single communication could obliterate others' knowing of the mother, even where, for example, the communication conveys a paucity of propositional or qualitative knowledge. Secondly, the voluntariness condition can be understood both in a positive and negative sense. Typically, the videos would

---

[25] Lindemann (2014).

[26] Ibid, Abstract.

[27] Ibid, xiv.

[28] I am grateful to Professor Jonathan Herring for raising this objection.

convey propositional and qualitative knowledge about the mother, which she intended specifically for the child—this is the positive sense. But this also means that she did not intend any new knowledge for others. If we take the voluntariness condition seriously, their knowing must persist. Even if the information conveyed to the child had a private, secret quality to it, we might still expect a threshold to be satisfied if old knowing were to be displaced. Hence, because the videos were not intended for those others, it means that at the time there was a mind to be known, it was known *as, and to the extent that,* she wanted them to know it. In other words, new knowing need not destroy old knowing. Rather, old knowing may persist for as long as there is no new knowing that is, or would be, available and intended *for them.*

In light of the above analysis, the theory can now be refined. The requirement for *no new knowing* is superfluous once we factor in whom the information is *for*. This produces a more plausible theory. First, it resolves the over-demandingness of the 'no new knowing' condition, which can be satisfied by minimal conditions of knowing. Secondly, it brings out the significance of voluntary agency, which should capture the sense in which a person both reveals and conceals information about who they are to others, as well as the limits of their ability to be known as they wish to be known.

7.5 Conclusion

It has been shown that you know someone personally, even where he or she is deceased, where you satisfy the conditions of personal knowing at the time personal knowing is possible. This resolves the putative paradox of *single-body* impersonation. P1 is known personally in the sense just described, whether or not we posit 'person stages' or 'selves' rather than persons. However, there remains the requirement for an intentional, deliberate act. This seems to be the natural idea of impersonation.[29] If P2 lacks an understanding that he is no longer P1, then clearly, he is not pretending or claiming to be anything. In the real world, there may be few scenarios in which a sufficiently extreme change in personal identity would be accompanied by the requisite cognitive awareness to satisfy the provision. This confirms that *mens rea* would not be satisfied and that mental disturbance cases, therefore, do not fit the theory. Nevertheless, Parfit's theory remains relevant in cases of extreme qualitative change, such as long-lost friends and amnesiacs, where deception occurs as between different selves within a single human life.

[29] I am grateful to Professor Jonathan Herring for pointing this out.

Cases

R v Elbekkay 1994 EWCA Crim 1, [1995] Crim LR 163

Legislation

Sexual Offences Act 2003, s. 76(2)(b)

References

Ali H, Fumerton R (2020) Knowledge by acquaintance vs. description. The Stanford encyclopedia of philosophy, Spring edn https://plato.stanford.edu/archives/spr2020/entries/knowledge-acquandescrip/
Benton M (2017) Epistemology personalized. Philos Q 67(269):813–834
Craig E (1991) Knowledge and the state of nature: an essay in conceptual synthesis. Clarendon Press, Oxford
Feldman R (2003) Epistemology. Prentice Hall foundations of philosophy series, Upper Saddle River
Harris LR (1976) Towards a consent standard in the law of rape. Univ Chic Law Rev 43(3): 613–644
Lindemann H (2014) Holding and letting go: The social practice of personal identities, Online edn. Oxford Academic. https://doi.org/10.1093/acprof:oso/9780199754922.001.0001
Matheson D (2010) Knowing persons. Dialogue Can Philos Rev 49(3):435–453
Parfit D (1984) Reasons and persons. Clarendon Press, Oxford
Talbert BM (2014) Knowing other people: a second-person framework. Ratio 28(2):190–206
Tarzia L, Fetherstonhaugh D, Bauer M (2012) Dementia, sexuality and consent in residential aged care facilities. J Med Ethics 38(10):609–613
Zagzebski L (2017) What is knowledge? In: Greco J, Sosa E (eds) The Blackwell guide to epistemology, pp 92–116

Chapter 8
Equivalence Thesis: Stage B

Equivalence Thesis (B): Fictitious Other Impersonation
P^1: It is impermissible to impersonate one's earlier self (per C^1)
P^2: Impersonating a fictitious person and impersonating one's earlier self are, other things equal, on a par in terms of permissibility
C^2: Therefore, impersonating a fictitious person is impermissible—let us call this *fictitious other impersonation*

8.1 Introduction

This chapter presents the second stage (B) of the Equivalence Thesis in relation to the case law on s. 76(2)(b) (the impersonation provision) of the Sexual Offences Act 2003. Specifically, it addresses impersonation of a fictitious person. It argues that if a defendant (D) creates a fictitious person whom he then pretends to be (a persona), thereby securing consent, the law should accept this as a legally effective deception even if there is no actual person in existence. This is so for moral reasons. The law should not allow the victim (V) to be worse off the more effectively she is deceived.

The law's approach to fictitious persons will be illustrated by reference to *R v Devonald*.[1] This case concerned deception as to purpose under s. 76(2)(a) of the 2003 Act (2003). The facts are that an adult male had created a fake online profile as a teenage girl to deceive the victim, his daughter's ex-boyfriend, into performing a sexual act over the internet. His true purpose was to humiliate the victim for mistreating his daughter, not mutual sexual gratification. The case was not adjudicated as a case of deception as to identity due to the common law's restrictive approach to s. 76(2)(b) (the impersonation provision). Only real (existing) persons

[1] [2008] EWCA Crim 527.

R. Farah, *Rereading Identity Deception in the UK Sexual Offences Act 2003*, SpringerBriefs in Law, https://doi.org/10.1007/978-3-031-44475-3_8

can be objects of impersonation, whereas D had assumed 'the identity of a non-existent girl'.[2] In what follows, however, I analyse this case in terms of impersonation to explore the explanatory value this offers.

8.2 The Problem of Fictitious Persons

The problem is that where D pretends to be a fictitious character—in this case, 'Cassey'—the 'person' element is not satisfied. This was surely incorrect, as a relationship conducted online is not obviously incapable of satisfying the 'known personally' requirement of s. 76(2)(b).[3] As Simester et al. point out, there is no reason to require physical acquaintance if we understand the reference to 'personally' properly. Whether or not V and D met 'in person,' that is, face to face, we should take 'personally' to include 'reference to D as an individual person (as distinct from others).'[4] Instead, this case was adjudicated under s. 76(2)(a), as a deception 'as to nature or purpose' case. Although the offence in this case was causing a person to engage in sexual activity without consent under s. 4 of the 2003 Act, the law on consent is the same as that which applies to rape under s. 1.

Devonald illustrates the judicial failure to focus on the primary question: did V give consent to the person who was D? If not, then V necessarily consented to someone else, thereby satisfying the idea of impersonation. This failure leads to an absurdity, for it is not enough that D tells an untruth; that untruth must be, in addition, referentially true. Although it was a lie that the defendant was 'Cassey', it needed to be true that there was a person called 'Cassey' to satisfy the provision. There are two ways of capturing the flaw in this approach: (1) in terms of the failure to capture the effect of D's lies on V, and (2) in terms of the normative privilege the law affords D.

First, an analogy with *R v Jheeta*[5] may be helpful. Like *R v B*,[6] this case involved *fictitious other impersonation* and (fake) blackmail. Although V was subjected to threats and blackmail, she was not objectively at risk. However, crucially, the court looked at V's subjective experience, relying on the intense pressure she was under because D had lied to create the appearance of danger. Accordingly, it is not clear why the same (victim-centred) approach is not taken in respect of *fictitious other impersonation*. The blackmail in *Jheeta* was a fiction, just as the object of impersonation in several leading cases—Cassey in *Devonald*, Grant in *B*, the policeman in *Jheeta*—was a fiction. But what mattered was the effect of the lies on V. Treating

---

[2]Simester et al. (2016), p. 476.

[3]Stump (2010), p. 53.

[4]Simester et al. (2016), p. 477. Whilst I agree that this is among the meanings of 'personally,' I explore another meaning later in the chapter.

[5][2007] EWCA Crim 1699.

[6][2013] EWCA Crim 823.

Jheeta as a case of *fictitious other impersonation* would bring it within identity deception, assuming the argument in this chapter goes through. Applying these insights to identity deception, then, the question should be: was V taken in by D's deception, such that it caused her to agree to sex with D thinking he was someone else? Alternatively, did it cause her to agree to sex with D to satisfy the demands of the person D had pretended to be? Put simply, did D's impersonation enable him to secure sex with V that he could not have secured without his impersonation? Posing the questions in this way opens the door to very different outcomes in these cases.

Secondly, this approach is highly unsatisfactory where it endorses morally worse behaviour and makes a deceiver better off. The defendant in *Devonald* was engaged in a morally worse deception in at least one respect. He pretended not only that he was someone he was not, but also that there was a person called Cassey in existence. He was thereby engaged in two deceptions: (1) that there exists a person C and (2) that he is that person C. Yet, in such cases, the law (very generously for D) declines to recognise deception (1) because untrue. This, in turn, negates deception (2), which is rendered, because deception (1) disappears from the legal picture, legally impossible. This looks somewhat absurd. It means that if proposition (1) is true and you commit deception as to proposition (2), then you are caught by the provision. But if you decide to create a persona in relation to 1) so that V believes it to be true, followed by deception as to (2), you escape the clutches of the section. What a privileged position D is in!

8.3 Giving Legal Effect to D's Deception

The current legal approach entails a highly counterintuitive implication and misses what it normatively significant. It means that you are better off the worse you behave, whereas, as Gardner asserts in the context of consent, 'What seems to have true normative significance is that D succeeded in coercing V as he intended'.[7] It is surely relevant that he went to *extra* effort to make his deception effective; that he created a "tag team" of deceptions, as one might put it, to convince V. Should we not then hold him to his desired end where doing otherwise would be to V's detriment, particularly as he has shown himself to be *doubly* committed to it? Doing so would mean that if a defendant engages in deception of the second kind, and thereby secures consent, the law will not allow him to escape liability by having committed an earlier, more fundamental deception of the first kind—that was, moreover, aimed at making the second (operative) deception effective. Can the section reasonably accommodate such a reading?

A revised reading of the section would ask (a) whether D claimed to be someone else. Let us call this someone else '*supposed person*' (SP) to signify the fact that they

[7]Horder (1999), p. 106.

may not objectively exist. It would then ask (b) whether SP was known personally to V. And there seems no obvious reason why (b) should need to occur in advance of (a). Finally, it would ask (c) whether D succeeded in inducing V's consent by pretending to be SP. Such a reading would require a more expansive, contextual approach, which goes against the judiciary's tendency towards narrow conceptions—for example, in relation to autonomy or consent.[8] In respect of (b), it is accepted that it is not obvious that SP can be known personally due to the sense in which SP exists as an intrinsically deceptive entity. Although V is interacting with D-who-is-Cassey, V has no epistemic access to Cassey. However, it is assumed, *pace* both Matheson and Benton, that justified true belief is not required. This is for the same reasons as were given earlier. As Benton concedes, V certainly knows *someone* personally[9]—not least the fact that he is a deceiver. Thus, 'one person knows another just in case the first believes personal information about the second as a result of the second's having communicated the information specifically and manifestly to her'.[10] In sum, the provision remains intelligible under this amended reading.

To summarise this section, the 2003 Act is wrong to exclude impersonation of someone not known personally where D orchestrates the absence of personal knowing. As argued above, we should prevent V from faring worse under the law the worse D behaves. Other things equal, D's behaviour is morally worse where he does any of the following: commits multiple deceptions; creates fictitious persons (personas) whose existence V cannot reasonably verify;[11] threatens or pressurises V; continues his deception/s over a prolonged period. Both *Jheeta* and *B* fit this description. Plausibly, genuine consent is unthinkable in such circumstances. Yet, these cases were dealt with under s. 74, not s. 76, or even s. 75. The outcome may, of course, be the same. But the rationale of the cases matter and s. 74 depends on the findings of the jury, which leaves V vulnerable to the influence of rape myths and other misconceptions. Whereas it might be objected that online sexual activity, as occurred in *Devonald*, *Jheeta*, and *B*,[12] carries a presumption of *caveat emptor*, this is surely rebutted the better developed and executed D's deception/s, and the greater the contrast between D's identity and the object of his impersonation. Accordingly, I argue that there is moral equivalence between impersonating someone known personally and impersonating someone *not* known personally, which succeeds because of an *absence* of personal knowing for which D is responsible.

[8] Herring (2014).

[9] Benton (2017), p. 827.

[10] Matheson (2010), p. 434.

[11] Arguably, nor should she be expected to do so.

[12] And which can be expected to feature strongly in future cases given the proliferation of social media use.

8.4 Starting Points: A Reversal

This "victim-friendly" reading gains further support in light of the section's unstated assumption about starting points. In the context of assessing criminal liability, Gardner has pointed out that starting points matter to the outcome.[13] For Gardner, as for Honoré,[14] liability depends on what the actor did and brought about through his or her action. As he puts it:

> The first question, in all cases of culpability, is "what did the defendant do?" ... It is not "why does the mere fact that someone *happens to die* add to one's crime, or make a major crime out of an otherwise venal act?", but rather, "how does the mere fact that one kills accidentally serve to mitigate or otherwise intercede in the *wrongness of killing*?"[15]

This same logic may be applied to the impersonation provision. The problem with the original reading, as just outlined, was that it seemed to require that there be, first, a person whom V knows personally—and this person should exist (or have existed) *independently* of D. And, only second, that D has pretended to be said person. This rules out fictitious persons who do not exist independently of D's deception. But this misses what D actually did—the change he made in the world. D caused V to believe that he was a person he was not, so the consent is not *his*. Therefore, he has no good reason for the penetration.[16] That is the very essence of impersonation. One is left to wonder what difference it makes that a real other person was not in play. As shown earlier, the preparatory ruse is part and parcel of that. Because V was taken in by his deception, the act he performed must encompass this result. Thus, the question is not: Why does the mere fact that D engaged in an earlier ruse make an impersonation out of what is otherwise only a deception? Instead, the question is: How does the mere fact that 'Cassey' was D's creation intercede in the wrongness of impersonation?

It might be suggested that the relatively anonymous and casual nature of the sex means that, in *R v Melin*[17] terms, identity was not fundamental to the sexual encounter. Indeed, according to Kaufman's theory of 'thin' and 'thick' selves, this would seem to be an encounter where only thin selves were involved.[18] An analogy with mistaken identity in contract law illuminates this point. MacMillan observes that no mistake of identity occurs if the owner-seller 'would have dealt with anyone'.[19] Furthermore, there can be no mistake of identity where a rogue buyer assumes the identity of a fictitious person.[20] This is because, so MacMillan argues,

---

[13] Law Commission Report No. 237 (1996).

[14] Honoré (1999).

[15] Gardner (1996), para 4.37.

[16] Madden Dempsey and Herring (2007).

[17] [2019] EWCA Crim 557, [2019] QB 1063.

[18] Kaufman (2000), p. 94.

[19] MacMillan (2005), p. 711.

[20] Ibid, p. 742.

'Identity is not material, for if it were, he would have realized the fictitious nature of the identity.'[21] This analysis suggests that we can infer what is material, or fundamental, from what the victim pays attention to or cares about. However, it ignores the fact that the victim may be deceived into not paying attention at the time of consent to the thing she most cares about, as in R *(Monica) v DPP*,[22] where a sustained deception was involved. Even if the victim in *Devonald*[23] was engaged in a casual sexual encounter, it does not follow that identity was immaterial. The point is that whomever else he would have dealt with, he would *not* have dealt with the father of his ex-girlfriend.

8.5 A Continuum of Personal Knowing

This chapter has been discussing the challenge posed by *fictitious other impersonation*. Having critically analysed the law's restrictive approach to impersonation as this relates to the *object* of impersonation, I now sketch a further argument. This focuses on a different aspect of the 'personal knowing' condition within the impersonation provision.[24] While Simester et al. observe that the meaning of 'personally' includes reference to someone as a distinct individual, here I focus on personal knowing in terms of proximity and remoteness. In what follows, I argue that this condition should be broadened to include (a) negative dimensions of personal knowing and (b) stronger and weaker versions of it.

In several cases, someone whom V knew personally pretended to be someone whom V did not know personally. This is the inverse of the formulation in s. 76(2)(b). I refer to this as the 'negative dimension'. The current approach does not include this dimension. Equally, personal knowing can be understood in stronger and weaker terms. In several cases, we see these different strengths of personal knowing in action. But again, the law does not take such nuance into account, restricting its meaning to direct experience of the person and making no differentiation based on how superficial that experience is.

Instead of this rather crude approach, I argue that we should imagine the condition of personal knowing as a continuum. I offer only a rough sketch here, but we can posit four senses: (1) Knowing someone intimately, (2) Knowing someone personally, (3) Being intimately acquainted with someone, and (4) Being basically (roughly) acquainted with someone. I locate 'knowing of someone' and 'not knowing someone personally' outside of the continuum. Despite this continuum implying a more expansive and variable concept of personal knowing, the impersonation provision recognises only (2): knowing personally. Yet, some of the sexual offences

[21] Ibid, p. 742.

[22] [2018] EWHC 3508 (Admin), [2019] QB 1019.

[23] *Devonald* (n 1).

[24] Per s 76(2)(b), SOA 2003.

case law concerns personal knowing in one or more of the above senses. And indeed, some of these senses may be interrelated. Senses (3) and (4) are weaker senses of personal knowing, while (1) is a stronger sense of personal knowing. Moreover, there are several cases of D pretending to be someone whom V *did not know* personally. This is the negative sense of personal knowing mentioned above. Several questions arise: Might some of these senses of personal knowing be normatively significant? Is there reason to bring the absence of personal knowing within the continuum? And if we think these additional senses capture neglected aspects of the wrong of identity deception, can the impersonation provision be reformulated to accommodate them?

To help answer these questions, let us return to *Devonald.* I suspect that this case reflects several aspects of the continuum, depending on how we define them. One possibility is that it involves (2) and either (3) or (4). For the sake of argument, let us assume that prior to the offence, V had had some contact with D, his ex-girlfriend's father. And let us define online interactions as acquaintance-based senses of personal knowing—whether basic or intimate. Accordingly, we can frame *Devonald* as a case of someone whom V knew personally pretending to be someone with whom V was merely either basically acquainted (given the casual and/or superficial nature of the conversation) or intimately acquainted (given their intimate, sexually charged conversation). Alternatively, if V had only knowledge of the father, then this implies a different set of senses of personal knowing. Although there is not space to develop a fully worked account of this, including the normative significance of the interrelatedness of these difference senses,[25] incorporating this continuum of personal knowing is important if we are to reflect the complexity and multiplicity of the wrong of sexual deception.

R v Jheeta and *R v B* are additional illustrations of the continuum I have outlined. In both these cases, D was V's boyfriend. Therefore, she knew him intimately. Yet, he pretended to be someone whom she did not know personally. One can imagine the distress and sense of betrayal upon learning that what one thought was casual, anonymous sex was, in fact, shared with someone whom V knew intimately (sense 1), as in *B*. The opposite is also true. The paradigm case is where V is tricked into thinking she is having sex with someone she knows intimately but whom she, in fact, knows only personally, or as an acquaintance, or not at all.[26] *Jheeta* is slightly different from *B*, in that V knew it was her boyfriend (seemingly estranged) that she was having sex with. However, she was deceived into believing that she was doing so to satisfy the demands of someone she did not know personally, and whom D had pretended to be as part of his wider ruse. The truth is that she was having sex to satisfy the demands of someone she knew intimately, who was the same person she

[25] For example, there might be little wrong with deception that corresponds to points close to each other on the continuum, such as (1) and (2), but far more wrong with pretending not to know someone while, in fact, knowing them intimately—point (1) on the continuum and non-personal knowing, which is outside of the continuum.

[26] Although the provision does not reflect this nuance in terms of degrees of personal knowing.

was having sex with. More will be said about this in Chap. 10—Concluding Remarks.

8.6 Conclusion

It has been shown that fictitious persons can be objects of impersonation (*fictitious other impersonation*). The argument was developed through discussion of *Devonald*,[27] which tested the judicial approach to deception. Although this case concerned deception as to purpose, it is more plausibly read as an identity case. This was supplemented by moral argument. I identified two separate deceptions carried out by D and then suggested we rethink our starting points to reflect the normative significance of his conduct. It was shown that the law should give legal effect to D's first deception, thereby ensuring that he is accountable for his second. In parallel, the condition of 'personal knowing' in the impersonation provision was critically analysed, and objections answered. Specifically, I argued that we should think of personal knowing as a continuum involving positive and negative dimensions, as well as stronger and weaker versions. In the next chapter, it is argued that *fictitious other impersonation* is equivalent to *fictitious self impersonation* even where this involves fabrication of only a few personal traits/attributes.

Reports

Law Commission, *Legislating the criminal code: Involuntary manslaughter* (Law Com No 237, 1996) (London: HMSO)

Legislation

Sexual Offences Act 2003, s. 76(2)(b)

Cases

R v B [2013] EWCA Crim 823
R v Jheeta [2007] EWCA Crim 1699
R (Monica) v DPP [2018] EWHC 3508 (Admin), [2019] QB 1019

[27] *Devonald* (n 1).

R v Devonald [2008] EWCA Crim 527
R v Melin [2019] EWCA Crim 557, [2019] QB 1063

References

Benton M (2017) Epistemology personalized. Philos Q 67(269):813–834

Gardner J (1996). In: Law Commission. Legislating the criminal code: involuntary manslaughter (Law Com No 237, 1996). HMSO, London, paras 4.37–4.38 https://lawcom.gov.uk/app/uploads/2015/03/lc237_Legislating_the_Criminal_Code_Involuntary_Manslaughter.pdf

Herring J (2014) Rape and the definition of consent. Natl Law Sch India Rev 26(1):62–76

Honoré AM (1999) Responsibility and Fault. Bloomsbury Publishing

Horder J (1999) Consent, threats and deception in criminal law. King's Law J 10(1):104–108

Kaufman F (2000) Thick and thin selves: reply to Fischer and Speak. Midwest Stud Philos 24:94–97

MacMillan C (2005) Rogues, swindlers and cheats: the development of mistake of identity in English contract law. Camb Law J 64(3):711–744

Madden Dempsey M, Herring J (2007) Why sexual penetration requires justification. Oxf J Leg Stud 27(3):467–491

Matheson D (2010) Knowing persons. Dialogue Can Philos Rev 49(3):435–453

Simester AP, Spencer JR, Stark F, Sullivan GR, Virgo GJ (2016) Simester and Sullivan's criminal law: theory and doctrine, 6th edn. Hart

Stump E (2010) Wandering in darkness: narrative and the problem of suffering. Oxford University Press

Chapter 9
Equivalence Thesis: Stage C

Equivalence Thesis (C): Fictitious Self Impersonation
P¹: It is impermissible to impersonate a fictitious other person (*fictitious other impersonation*) (per C²)
P²: Pretending to be a different *kind* of person and *fictitious other impersonation* are, other things equal, on a par in terms of permissibility
[P² is established by means of the Substantial Difference Argument][1]
C³: Therefore, pretending to be a different kind of person is impermissible—let us call this fictitious self impersonation

9.1 Introduction

It will now be shown that impersonating a fictitious other person (fictitious other impersonation) may be equivalent to pretending to be a different *kind* of person (fictitious self impersonation). In the former case, one creates and adopts an entire persona, as in *R v Devonald*.[2] In the latter, one fabricates (or denies) not an entire persona but individual traits or attributes.[3] It is argued that there is no good reason to prohibit one but not the other. I will defend this view against the objection that fabricating a single trait does not involve enough change to count as impersonation.

[1] This is formulated later in this chapter.

[2] [2008] EWCA Crim 527.

[3] This is a matter of degree. As I understand this, there are two possibilities for fictitious impersonation. One might fabricate an entire self. This is equivalent to adopting a persona. It is fictitious other impersonation. Alternatively, one might fabricate individual traits/attributes, not amounting to an entire persona or self. One the face of it, this would not amount to impersonation. Thus, the central argument is that properly understood, deception as to traits can amount to fictitious self impersonation.

R. Farah, *Rereading Identity Deception in the UK Sexual Offences Act 2003*, SpringerBriefs in Law, https://doi.org/10.1007/978-3-031-44475-3_9

It argues, first, that a single trait/attribute can engender substantial effects over a person's lifetime; and secondly, that traits bleed into identity. This latter point reflects the direction of the empirical literature that was discussed at the outset of the book. As these claims overlap, they will be addressed together. The thesis is underpinned by a moral assumption, which mirrors the reasoning in Chap. 8 that we should give legal effect either to D's deception or to what this logically entails. Thus, we have reason to treat D as claiming to be the person he would have been had the trait/attribute, which he deceptively claimed, been genuine. Should D wish to avoid this moral constraint, he need only tell the truth.

9.2 Identity, Attributes and Qualities: A Continuum

The starting point for this part of the discussion is that rather than a bright-line distinction between properties of the person and identity, there is, more plausibly, a continuum—with individual traits/attributes at one end, hardening gradually into a stable core that is one's identity at the other. Indeed, in R (*Monica) v DPP*,[4] it was noted that 'There may be subtle metaphysical distinctions... between "identity", "attributes" and "qualities"'.[5] The assumption of a bright-line between the internal and the external is, as Radin observes, 'traceable to the prevailing world view that posits persons as subjects in a world of objects'.[6] Various identity theorists are critical of this assumption,[7] and some deny that there exists a stable, immutable core at all.[8] On the most extreme versions of relational theory, for example, there simply is no self. However, such theories are controversial, and they do not address the role of identity as a *social category*, by which people are often constrained. Instead, positing a continuum, it is at least clear that the Sexual Offences Act 2003 is not drawing the line in the right place. While there is not space to explore precisely where the line should be drawn, the law has failed to justify (a) why it requires an extreme difference between D and the object of his impersonation, and (b) why it rejects as a candidate for extreme difference the very fact that one person is a sexual deceiver and 'the other' is not.

Defending the bright-line distinction between traits/attributes and identity, Tadros asserts, 'The identity of a person or nature of an act is robust',[9] such that the identity of a person is unchanged by the properties of that person. On this basis, V has still consented to D '∅-ing'. Although Tadros considers this view to be metaphysically sound, he concedes that there is a moral argument for holding consent to be invalid

[4][2018] EWHC 3508 (Admin), [2019] QB 1019.

[5]Ibid, [82].

[6]Radin (1987), p. 1909.

[7]Ibid.

[8]Meyers (2000); Taylor (1995).

[9]Tadros (2016), p. 247.

where D deceives V about the *properties* he has. This concession is unsatisfactory, however, given that there is both a better metaphysical view *and* a complementary moral argument. Radin proposes an alternative view of personhood, in which a wide range of particulars, including a person's politics, religion, sexuality, experiences, moral commitments, character and personal attributes, is seen as integral to the self.[10] Accordingly, the same person may not remain when a given particular is subtracted.[11] In support of this claim, it will be argued that having different traits/attributes involves a different lived experience, through one's interaction in the physical and social worlds, which can fundamentally alter who one is as a person. This is the Substantial Difference Argument, which is sketched below.

9.3 Substantial Difference Argument

P1: Small differences in traits/attributes can generate substantial differences in persons in a qualitative sense
P2: If you had the trait/attribute, you would have been substantially different as a person **[This follows via the Counterfactual View]**
P3: To claim different traits/attributes is to claim to be the substantially different person you would have been
[This follows via a moral assumption that imputes a secondary intention to D. Thus, to intend deception as to qualitative identity is to intend what this logically entails][12]
C: Therefore, deception as to traits/attributes and qualitative impersonation are, other things equal, on a par in terms of impermissibility

This argument is that deception about a trait/attribute may be equivalent to deception about identity in a qualitative sense where the following counterfactual is true: **If D had a given trait/attribute, D would have been substantially different as a person**. It follows that by claiming the trait/attribute, D claims to be the (substantially different) person he would have been had he possessed the trait/attribute. Crucially, as before, we give legal effect to what this logically entails—the person he would have been. This is for normative reasons. Thus, we treat him as claiming to be that substantially different person.

Before examining this argument more closely, I want to recall Chap. 6, which demonstrated the various ways in which the Substantial Difference argument has

[10] Radin (1987), p. 1906.
[11] Ibid, p. 1906.
[12] Further argument would be needed to address this *mens rea* element. I leave aside questions about the justice of imputed intention in criminal law.

theoretical support. I drew on the work of Charles Taylor and Kathleen Wallace in support of a dynamic, socio-relational approach to identity change. We saw that Taylor situates the person contextually, in relational, political, and moral space. The question of identity is thus bound up with the idea of one's orientation. Kathleen Wallace proposed a relational, network theory of personal identity. We saw that she posited a plurality of selves, or persons, united in a complex and highly variable system of interrelated traits. Together, these accounts provide a useful analytical lens within which to rethink the nature of qualitative identity change.

Further support is provided by the concept of integrity.[13] Various theorists distinguish this concept, as psychological, from that of identity, which they characterise as ontological.[14] We saw in Chap. 5 that the matter is more complex, however, and the dichotomy between numerical and qualitative identity has been challenged. Indeed, Noggle concedes that a theory could treat integrity as necessary and sufficient for diachronic identity.[15] Nevertheless, the orthodox understanding of integrity is that certain particulars are integral to the self. Wallace's account of traits, which vary in terms of their relevance, appeals to this idea. In a similar vein, Noggle argues that desires bear different relationships to the self. As he explains, some, but not all, 'seem to be central to shaping me as the particular person I am, making me the person who is leading the particular life I am leading.'[16] This recalls the characterisation question, which asks whether the characteristics that shape and given meaning to a human life have survived.[17] Integrity, then, is a psychological notion centring on what the individual cares about, how they see themselves as a person, what concerns animate their life, and so on.

In advancing his desire-based theory of well-being, Noggle makes an interesting claim, which mirrors the idea of substantial difference to which I appeal. He notes that when someone becomes 'radically different' psychologically, this changes who they are as a person, such that they suffer a loss of integrity.[18] The person's psychological identity will have changed, and this will cause the person to have difficulty identifying with their changed self.[19] This suggests that lack of identification, or repudiation, is a proxy for substantial difference. While helpful, there are two points to make here. First, it seems to imply that only moral deterioration, not moral improvement, can ground psychological identity change (or loss of integrity). Although this aligns with the 'moral self effect' discussed in Chap. 5, it seems both arbitrary and idealised. It implies that human lives have a positive arc towards moral improvement, indeed, towards our true, higher selves. This might

[13] Noggle (1999); Schechtman (2018). See also Wallace (2019) who modifies Buchler's (1990) use of the concept.

[14] Noggle (1999), p. 315.

[15] Ibid, p. 315.

[16] Ibid, p. 315.

[17] Schechtman (2018).

[18] Noggle (1999), p. 315.

[19] Ibid, p. 315.

be true. Certainly, lay intuitions think it is.[20] Indeed, it might be said to mirror the teleological understanding of nature as evolving towards the good. But equally, there may be no coherent trajectory. Our lives may just as well be an ever-oscillating pendulum between moral goodness and moral badness. We may even become less moral or virtuous as we mature. For this reason, it seems more likely that the salience of moral deterioration reflects what matters most to people and the fact that people react most strongly when community values are threatened.[21] Furthermore, this suggests that the more useful concept is non-recognition, rather than repudiation, as the marker for identity change; for this would capture moral change in either direction.

Secondly, and relatedly, we should reject the focus on the individual's self-perception in determining identity change. Because Noggle proposes a desire-based theory of well-being, he must adopt the subjective perspective. By contrast, I propose a subjective-objective hybrid approach. Accordingly, on the one hand, I allow for an objective assessment of the kind of change that should count, such as major change to a hub. Secondly, I centre the perspectives of other relevant persons. Thus, loss of integrity/psychological identity change would depend not on my reaction to the changed version of myself, but on those with whom I am meaningfully related. Thus, whether there is, or should be, a failure of recognition would signal the necessary degree of change. Crucially, this would also reflect the significance of recognition, per Taylor and Honneth, in identity formation and reformation.

9.3.1 *Counterfactual View*

The critic might take issue with the second premise of the Substantial Difference Argument above. This claim is doing a lot of argumentative work, and it is open to question whether the proposed counterfactual is sound. The next section will defend this premise.

The obvious objection is that the argument works where there is wholesale deception by D about his traits/attributes, but not where D simply substitutes one or two so as to secure V's consent. Clearly, where wholesale deception occurs, this is equivalent (imagining this occurring in a diachronic sense) to there being a significant reduction in connectedness between D and the self he presents. Without difficulty, we can imagine saying, as Parfit puts it, 'It was not *I* who did that, but an earlier self'.[22] As Tobia puts it, this commonplace intuition is traceable to the view that 'a certain magnitude of dissimilarity breaks personal identity.'[23] It has

[20] Chen and Urminsky (2022).

[21] Everett et al. (2022).

[22] Parfit (1986), p. 352.

[23] Tobia (2015), p. 402.

already been shown that we can treat deception as to an earlier (or imagined) self like deception as to another person. Equally, looking at this issue through the *Network of Selves in Moral-Relational Space* (Wallace-Taylor) lens, such wholesale deception is likely to track loss of or change to a hub. But what about where only one or two traits are involved? The intuition is that there has not been *enough* change to count—that D must be substantially the *same* person. In Tobia's terms, it lacks the requisite 'magnitude of dissimilarity' that would break the identity relation.[24] But there are two replies here. The first is that this fails to appreciate that a single trait/attribute can entail substantial change in a qualitative sense over time. The Wallace-Taylor lens can explain this. Secondly, insofar as identity is a *social category*, it may be enough that society generally thinks the trait important. I will explore each of these assertions below.

A dynamic and socio-relational[25] theory of identity suggests that individual traits/attributes may play a significant role in identity, such that inter-subjective phenomena shape development of a person's identity.[26] Accordingly, we should not think of a single attribute/trait as simply added or removed like a puzzle piece—or that doing so is without consequence. Various commentators confirm this richer, more nuanced view. Thus, Clifford posits identity not as a 'boundary to be maintained but as a nexus of relations and transactions actively engaging a subject'.[27] In a similar vein, Wendt posits social identities as 'at once cognitive schemas that enable an actor to determine 'who I am/we are' in a situation and positions in a social role structure of shared understandings and expectations'.[28] Foster and Herring echo this view, suggesting that the boundary of the individual is 'porous and fluid'[29]—a description that reflects a relational, communitarian model of the person. As they put it, 'Our shape... is a function of the pressure of others'.[30] And for Feinberg, 'The individual is a social being through and through, and much of what we think of as essential in him is inconceivable without his relations'.[31] This means, per Taylor, that '[O]ur identity is never simply defined in terms of our individual properties. It also places us in some social space'.[32] Hence, only by considering where a person sits within their social nexus can one truly understand who that individual is.

The above exposition suggests that one's traits/attributes are of fundamental importance, engendering a unique, lived experience with dynamic and extensive intrapersonal effects. Consider the following examples related to wealth/class belonging, group membership, and race.

---

[24] Ibid, p. 396.

[25] Meyers (2000).

[26] Relational theorists make a similar claim in respect of autonomy. See Wardrope (2015).

[27] Clifford (1988), p. 344.

[28] Wendt (1994), p. 395.

[29] Foster and Herring (2017), p. 3.

[30] Ibid, p. 3.

[31] Feinberg (1990), p. 85.

[32] Taylor (1995), p. 62.

9.3.1.1 Wealth and Class Belonging

To be a wealthy man is not simply to have money; it is to have the lived experience of a wealthy man. He will have the class belonging of a wealthy man, the values, tastes, and attitudes of a wealthy man. Indeed, it was this concern that motivated Parfit's example of the young Russian.[33] As he interacts within his social circle, he will develop his worldview in accordance with that experience. His empirical self will 'arise within conversation'.[34] Perhaps, instead, he will reject the values associated with his status. What matters is that he will form values in keeping with his interpretation of his own identity and his nature.[35] This aligns with Taylor's notion of one's orientation in moral space.[36] This may cause him to form new group identities, or to engage in 'piecemeal synthesis and provisional reconstruction'[37] of old ones. His self will form and reform. His friendships and associations will further shape him—and in a different way from those friendships and associations to which he does not have access. These are, as Sandel puts it, his '"community allegiances"—those more or less enduring attachments and commitments which taken together define the person I am'.[38] As Berlin notes, 'My independent self is not something which I can detach from my relationship with others, or from those attributes of myself which consist in their attitude towards me'.[39] Therefore, the self is inescapably interdependent.

Our new framework is useful here. I suggest that class membership (for which wealth may be a proxy) is a sub-network or hub in Wallace's terms.[40] Parfit's example of the young Russian socialist illuminates this issue. In his example, the Russian wanted to guard against the possibility that he would lose his ideals once he inherited vast wealth in later years. Parfit explains that the Russian man says to his wife, 'I regard my ideals as essential to me. If I lose these ideals, I want you to think that I cease to exist. I want you to regard your husband then, not as me, the man who asks you for this promise, but only as his corrupted later self.'[41] Does this tell us anything meaningful about personal identity? I think there are two observations to make.

First, this passage conveys an essential relational dimension. It seems relevant that the man is speaking to his wife with whom he is intimately related. On Taylor's theory, such an intimate relationship is part of one's self-definition. The young Russian refers to himself as a husband, a man, and a self. In positioning himself as

[33] Parfit (1984).

[34] Ibid, p. 64.

[35] Anderson and Honneth (2005); Westlund (2009).

[36] Taylor (1995).

[37] Meyers (2000), p. 163.

[38] Sandel (1982), p. 179.

[39] Berlin (1969), p. 159.

[40] Wallace (2019).

[41] Parfit (1984), p. 327.

an internal multiplicity—as an 'I', a 'me', and a 'he'—he also positions himself as a 'who I am *to you*'—a self in the world of others. This positioning aligns with dialogical self-theory (DST), in which the self can be explained only in relation to the other.[42] Thus, we are at once 'self-in-other' and 'other-in-self'.[43] I think this helps to address the problem of identity change. 'Who' or 'what' the man is depends, in part, on his significant relationships.

Secondly, at first blush, the passage seems to confirm the moral self-effect. But this rather begs the question as to those ideals or values deemed morally superior. Instead, we should view this as a concern about change to *self-agency*, whereby different social interactions generate different positioning, counter-positioning, and, ultimately, different intentions.[44] In expressing the importance he attaches to his ideals, he is engaged in second-order volitions, per Frankfurt,[45] or strong evaluation, per Taylor.[46] This valuing of ideals remains true of him. Thus, I think it matters less that ideals change than that an ideal is lost without being replaced by a commensurate ideal. In Taylor's terms, we can describe this as orientation in moral space,[47] which requires no particular conception of the good. Indeed, someone who was a socialist and became a capitalist has replaced one political ideology with another. Both may be reasonably endorsed and rationalised. Both the young and the old Russian may be equally committed to living according to their respective ideologies. Whether we think there has been change of the right kind, or to the right degree, surely depends on the dynamic interrelationship of associated traits, per Wallace, and the impact on defining relationships, per Taylor.

9.3.1.2 Race

Although race is plausibly a social construct, it often coincides with cultural differences that shape the person in unique and distinctive ways. Intersectionality, an analytic lens for theorising identity and oppression, lends further support to this argument.[48] As Anthias defines it, 'intersectionality posits that social divisions interrelate in terms of the production of social relations and in terms of people's lives.'[49] Such interrelationality necessarily entails significant complexity. Yet, some commentators contend that the law should not protect conditional consent when it is based on morally objectionable reasons. For example, Williams identifies reasons

[42] Gallagher and Marcel (1999).

[43] Epilogue, p. 492.

[44] Gallagher and Marcel (1999).

[45] Frankfurt (1971).

[46] Taylor (1995).

[47] Ibid.

[48] Views differ concerning what 'intersectionality' refers to. See Anthias (2012) for discussion.

[49] Anthias (2012), p. 2.

that are 'potentially socially undesirable,[50] such as anti-Semitism or racism. Clement suggests that the criminal law should not legitimise harmful attitudes.[51] With respect, this view is unconvincing, for two main reasons.

First, the principle of sexual autonomy guarantees a woman's right to regulate access to her intimate parts for any reason whatsoever. Yet, where deception occurs, the moral quality of her reasoning is subject to scrutiny. This implies a view of women in which they are (or should be) available for sexual penetration unless having good reason to refuse. But the opposite is true. There are many reasons against sex, given the significant and asymmetric risks it poses for women[52]—not least her susceptibility to being deceived. Thus, the man who seeks to sexually penetrate her must provide countervailing reasons. Secondly, it subjects V to moral scrutiny from which D is spared. As Williams observes in *R v Cuerrier*,[53] the Supreme Court of Canada declined to allow D's lies, though 'immoral and reprehensible,'[54] to result in a rape conviction.[55] Yet, any moral disvalue underlying V's conditional consent seems to be relevant. Furthermore, it is problematic that the law does not protect racially motivated reasoning about consent where V is tricked, but it does protect such reasoning where she is, for example, forced. It seems wrong for such an important issue to depend on which tactic D happens to use to (illegitimately) secure consent. In both cases, D has failed to respect V's reasons. He has failed to respect her autonomy. This is the core of the wrong. The method used—threat, force, non-disclosure, deception—may simply not matter. Indeed, it might be better to treat methods as aggravating factors causing different harms. Moreover, the law allows D (by his choice of means) to determine V's normative status in respect of the law. The law should simply say: D commits rape where he violates V's autonomy whether by ignoring, removing, or creating reasons.[56]

9.3.1.3 Group Identity

Group identities may be especially important for this question of change, for example with religious identities. This is because of the fusion of individual and collective aspects, as well as the nature of the core beliefs of the identity.[57] The same must be true of ideology-based social identities, such as socio-political activism. It has been observed that a strong personal commitment to a group may lead people to

---

[50] Williams (2008), p. 67.

[51] Clement (2018), p. 276.

[52] Madden Dempsey and Herring (2007).

[53] [1998] 2 S.C.R. 371; [1998] 162 D.L.R. (4th).

[54] Ibid, [563].

[55] Williams (2008), p. 67.

[56] *Creation* of reasons might be less morally wrongful. Still, depending on the facts, it could come within the offence, though perhaps as a second-degree version of rape.

[57] See Ysseldyk (2017); Ysseldyk et al. (2010, 2018).

endorse normative beliefs, which direct how one thinks one ought to think or behave.[58] This links to social constructionist theory. De Cecco and Elias capture the idea thus: 'For the constructionists, community becomes reified and confers personal identity. Identity begets ideology which, in turn, dictates individual decision.'[59] Thus, someone who is religious might be against extra-marital sex, or have conservative values related to reproduction. They may have certain social or other traits traceable to this identity. The better interpretation of *Monica*[60] is that D represented himself as having an ideology-based identity, which, had it been true, would have placed him in direct conflict with his identity as a police officer and authority figure. Thus, it is not simply that he concealed his occupation. As part of his deception, he will have concealed related traits, such as respect for authority, compliance with the law, opposition to activism, and so on. Indeed, perhaps he even held an underlying hostility to, or contempt for V, which has relational significance. At the very least, it is suggested that D's pursuit of V as part of a police operation contradicts his identity as a sexual partner to V.

Of course, we can think of a group identity that seems more trivial, such as being a football fan. We can imagine D deceiving V about the team he supports, knowing that V is a fan of that team and makes his support a condition of her consent. Might this amount to an unlawful deception as to identity? Intuitively, it seems unlikely. But I think it depends. We might consider it a strongly relevant trait (in Wallace's terms) if D supported the archrivals of V's team. Perhaps the teams' rivalry reflects divisive political-religious heritage, such that particular properties and relations are so salient that their presence or absence tracks substantial (qualitative) difference. The point is that even seemingly trivial traits can matter a great deal, even on an objective account of 'mattering'.[61] The Wallace-Taylor lens, like the socio-relational account in general, may not produce clear answers. But that is a function of the complexity and variability of the system that is the person.

Consequently, a single trait or attribute, seemingly inconsequential on its own, may have a significant ripple effect in respect of identity in a qualitative sense. As Foster and Herring point out in respect of memories, some attributes 'seem to go to *what* we are, not just *how* we are'.[62] That is, they may be attributes, but they are not *mere* attributes. The distinction between traits/attributes and identity is, in other words, academic in light of the ability of those traits/attributes to be 'determinative of what we are'.[63] Therefore, to hold, as in *Monica*, that occupation was not a fundamental aspect of identity,[64] neglects the sense in which non-fundamental

[58] Duckitt (1989), p. 70.

[59] De Cecco and Elia (1993), p. 18.

[60] *Monica* (n 4).

[61] This all assumes an objective account. On a subjective account, the conditions V places on her consent express what matters (to her).

[62] Foster and Herring (2017), p. 18.

[63] ibid, p. 18.

[64] *Monica* (n 4).

aspects can have fundamental effects—and it should not matter that they do so in a non-linear, seemingly indiscernible manner.

9.3.2 *Objection from Unimportance*

It may be objected that a trait that is unimportant to D cannot plausibly be part of his identity. One can imagine a person who positively rejects any notion of race as a salient aspect of his or her identity. What, then, is the position where this aspect is nevertheless important to V? To answer this objection, a social constructivist account of identity has something to offer.

A social constructivist account understands identity as a social category, where social categories are understood as 'objective social facts beyond the reach of any one individual to change'.[65] To have an identity is just to 'assign oneself to a particular social category or perhaps just to be assigned to it by others'.[66] Importantly, the effect of the label must be to condition the way people behave or think.[67] Hence, an individual who rejects his or her identity will nevertheless be constrained by virtue of social convention and practice in his or her interactions with the world. As Herring explains, 'Our sense of self is a mixture of interlocking and sometimes conflicting social identities. We are not in reality free to 'live our lives as we choose' because we are constrained by the responsibilities, realities and relationships which embed our lives.'[68] Wallace's thesis lends support to this argument, as she argues that only some traits are chosen by the individual.[69] Moreover, Kahan et al. note the unconscious influence of group values and commitments on individuals' perception and reasoning, which are key drivers of action.[70] Therefore, it is at least clear on this account that D's personal view about a trait will not help him to avoid liability for deception in relation to it for as long as the trait has consequences in the world. Indeed, one might add that it is not only social categories that are socially constructed, but also our sense of ourselves as distinct individuals.[71] In this respect, whether claiming or rejecting a given trait, and in contradistinction to the Hobbesian view of the atomistic, autonomous self, D cannot escape the effect of a social process upon him.

The problem of unchosen traits and social categories arises clearly in cases of 'national identity impersonation'.[72] The Israel Supreme Court has adjudicated cases

[65] Fearon (1999).

[66] Ibid, p. 13.

[67] Ibid, p. 13.

[68] Herring (2013) on Nedelsky (1989).

[69] Wallace (2019), p. 29.

[70] Kahan et al. (2012).

[71] Fearon (1999), p. 16.

[72] Gross (2015).

of deception as to identity relating to nationality, although such cases might also be characterised in terms of race and/or religion.[73] In the *Kashur* case,[74] D had been convicted of rape by national identity impersonation. Alongside deception as to his personal status, he had pretended to be a Jew to secure the consent of a Jewish woman. An interesting perspective on this case is provided by Gross, who criticises the use of the criminal law to protect the 'dominant national-gender order.'[75] Thus, while he recognises the wrong perpetrated against the woman as an individual, he is concerned about the role of the Court in preventing people from rejecting socially constructed roles and from claiming more privileged identities.[76] There is a sense in which Gross' argument resembles the debate around the moral self-effect, in that, he is concerned about the direction of change. Thus, if a Jewish man had claimed a *less* privileged identity, such as pretending to be an Arab to secure consent with an Arab woman, it seems that Gross would be less concerned. Yet, whether people seek to enter more or less privileged identities does not alter the fact that the criminal law, in effect, by prohibiting such deception, maintains this boundary. Therefore, the better claim that Gross' argument invites us to consider is, more simply, that nationality of any kind should not be considered an important aspect of a person's identity. In reply, there are several points to make.

First, it is certainly true, as Gross points out, that gender, national, and other identities are 'performed' in social interaction. This reflects symbolic interactionism, discussed in Part II. Equally, we can accept the socially constructed nature of identities. It is thus reasonable to challenge the assumed stability and "naturalness" of identities, as Gross does.[77] Nevertheless, as discussed above, we cannot escape the influence of group identities on our perception, reasoning, normative beliefs, relationships, and responsibilities. Thus, claiming a particular national identity is a proxy for a whole range of traits that matter greatly to people, and which combine to make each person the distinct individual they are. Secondly, the idea that we should not treat national identity as important is belied by the very fact that D lied about it to secure consent. Thus, either it was very important to D, or he was aware that it was very important to V. Either way, the criminal law is right to prohibit it. This argument may not go through where, for example, D does not consider himself to be a deceiver in respect of the trait or identity and does not know that it is important to V, as may be argued in trans cases. Finally, while I am sympathetic to the intuition that people should be able to self-determine their identities, it is inevitable that the law should have the effect of preserving the dominant order, given that we expect law to reflect and protect shared community values. The alternative is to subordinate

[73] For example, CrimA 5734/10 Kashur v. state of Israel [2012], Takdin (Isr.), Nevo Legal Database.

[74] CrimC (Jer) 561/08 State of Israel v. Sabbar Kashur, PM 1996(123) (2010) (Isr.).

[75] Gross (2015).

[76] Ibid, p. 33.

[77] Ibid, p. 3.

the sexual autonomy of women to the pursuit of social-moral ideals. However desirable these might be, it is not for women to bear this burden.

There is a related objection. Where a trait is not important to society generally, does it lie beyond the scope of this thesis? Not necessarily, for a further reply is available. This draws upon the idea that being a sexual deceiver is the kind of trait/attribute that means D is a substantially different person to the one he presents. Sexual relationships, paradigmatically, involve vulnerability, and trust is required of sexual partners. Surely, willingness to subject another person to deceptive sex indicates a significant difference in character relative to someone unwilling to do such a thing? We should recall Benson's theory of 'the unthinkable' here,[78] which suggests that what we are unwilling to do is a marker for identity. Equally, we saw in Chap. 5 how a person's commitments might be identity-defining.[79] D may object here on the basis that to have deceived on one occasion does not make him a deceiver generally. However, this ignores the independent significance of choice. A useful analogy may be drawn with Honoré's work on responsibility and luck in the criminal law context.[80] Outcome responsibility is argued to be inescapable, being a counterpart and a constituent of personal identity and character. Hence, when we choose to act to bring about a consequence in the world, we partly constitute ourselves by this choice. As a result, there is good reason to reject the 'analytical separation of the subject's identity from his actions and commitments as a member of a particular social world'.[81] If choices have this significance, then the choice itself to deceive may come within an identity analysis, without needing to interrogate either the content of that choice or its relative importance to D, or to society generally.

This conclusion has somewhat unappealing implications. As noted in Chap. 6, it seems to commit us to the position that any deception is an unlawful deception by virtue of D's misrepresentation of himself to V. This is so no matter how trivial his misrepresentation. As discussed earlier, I do not seek to draw this conclusion, and it is beyond the scope of this book to propose a counter-thesis. But it does seem possible to develop an account that would be acceptable. For example, we could focus on the idea of D's *self-concept*, and use this to distinguish lawful from unlawful deceptions. This might capture the significance of choice, while not committing to absolutism those inclined towards compromise. To get help with this account, we could appeal to the notion of critical interests, which Dworkin distinguishes from experiential interests.[82] Thus, we could hypothesise that D may not deceive V about his sense of who he is and the things that give his life value and meaning.

---

[78] Benson (2003).

[79] Archer (2015); Greenwood (1994).

[80] Honoré (1999).

[81] Ibid, p. 15.

[82] Dworkin (1993).

9.4 Conclusion

This chapter presented the final stage of the Equivalence thesis: that impersonation of a fictitious person is equivalent, morally speaking, to an individual pretending to be a different kind of person. This claim was supported by a Substantial Difference argument, grounded in a socio-relational understanding of the person. Thus, we have good reason to treat deception as to traits/attributes on a par with deception as to identity whenever who a person is undergoes sufficient change. The question of what constitutes sufficient change is difficult to resolve definitively. However, applying the Wallace-Taylor lens improves our understanding of the kinds of traits, influenced by social and other relations, that may have profound intrapersonal effects.

Cases

CrimC (Jer) 561/08 State of Israel v. Sabbar Kashur, PM 1996(123) (2010) (Isr.)
R v Devonald [2008] EWCA Crim 527
R (Monica) v DPP [2018] EWHC 3508 (Admin), [2019] QB 1019
R v Cuerrier [1998] 2 S.C.R. 371; [1998] 162 D.L.R. (4th)

Legislation

Sexual Offences Act 2003, s. 76(2)(b)

References

Anderson JH, Honneth A (2005) Autonomy, vulnerability, recognition, and justice. In: Christman J, Anderson J (eds) Autonomy and the challenges to liberalism: new essays. Cambridge University Press

Anthias F (2012) Intersectional what? Social divisions, intersectionality and levels of analysis. Ethinicities 0(0):1–17

Archer M (2015) The relational subject and the person: self, agent, and actor. In: Donati P, Archer M (eds) The relational subject. Cambridge University Press, pp 85–122

Benson C (2003) The unthinkable boundaries of self: the role of negative emotional boundaries in the formation maintenance and transformation of identities. In: Harre R, Moghaddam FM (eds) The self and others: positioning individuals in personal, political, and social contexts. Praegger/Greenwood

Berlin I (1969) Two concepts of liberty. In: Four essays on Liberty. Oxford University Press, pp 118–159. https://cactus.dixie.edu/green/B_Readings/I_Berlin%20Two%20Concpets%20of%20Liberty.pdf

Buchler J (1990) Metaphysics of natural complexes, 2nd edn. SUNY Press

Chen S, Urminsky O (2022) What's left of me? In: Tobia K (ed) Experimental philosophy of identity and the self. London, Bloomsbury, pp 71–85
Clement R (2018) Deception, mistake, privacy and consent: a conceptual framework for resolving the 'line-drawing' problem in sex-by-deception and mistaken sex. Dissertation, University of Oxford
Clifford J (1988) Identity in Mashpee. Harvard University Press, Cambridge
De Cecco JP, Elia JP (1993) If you seduce a straight person, can you make them gay?: Issues in biological essentialism versus social constructionism in gay and lesbian identities, vol 24(3–4). Psychology Press
Duckitt J (1989) Authoritarianism and group identification: a new view of an old construct. Polit Psychol 10(1):63–84
Dworkin R (1993) Life's dominion: an argument about abortion, euthanasia, and individual freedom. Vintage, New York
Everett J, Skorburg JA, Livingstone J (2022) Me, my (moral) self, and I. https://kar.kent.ac.uk/83701/1/Everett%20et%20al%20%282021%29%20Moral%20Self.pdf
Fearon JD (1999) What is identity (as we now use the word)? Unpublished manuscript, Stanford University, Stanford, pp 1–43. http://www.web.stanford.edu/group/fearon-research/cgi-bin/wordpress/wp-content/uploads/2013/10/What-is-Identity-as-we-now-use-the-word.pdf
Feinberg J (1990) Harmless wrongdoing: the moral limits of the criminal law, vol 4. Oxford University Press, Oxford
Foster C, Herring J (2017) Identity, personhood and the law. Springer Briefs in Law, Cham
Frankfurt HG (1971) Freedom of the will and the concept of a person. J Philos 68(1):5–20
Gallagher S, Marcel AJ (1999) The self in contextualized action. J Conscious Stud 6(4):4–30
Greenwood JD (1994) A sense of identity: prolegomena to a social theory of personal identity. J Theory Soc Behav 24(1):25–46
Gross A (2015) Rape by deception and the policing of gender and nationality borders. Tul J Law Sex 24:1–33
Herring J (2013) Forging a relational approach: best interests or human rights? Med Law Int 13(1): 3–97
Honoré AM (1999) Responsibility and fault. Bloomsbury Publishing
Kahan DM, Hoffman DA, Braman D, Evans D, Rachlinski JJ (2012) 'They saw a protest': cognitive illiberalism and the speech-conduct distinction. Stanford Law Rev 64:851–906
Madden Dempsey M, Herring J (2007) Why sexual penetration requires justification. Oxf J Leg Stud 27(3):467–491
Meyers DT (2000) Intersectional identity and the authentic self? Opposites attract! In: Mackenzie E, Stoljar N (eds) Relational autonomy. Oxford University Press
Nedelsky J (1989) Reconceiving autonomy: sources, thoughts and possibilities. Yale J Law Fem 1(1):7–36
Noggle R (1999) Integrity, the self, and desire-based accounts of individual good. Philos Stud 96(3):303–331
Parfit D (1984) Reasons and persons. Clarendon Press, Oxford
Parfit D (1986) What does matter. In: Reasons and persons. Clarendon Press, Oxford
Radin MJ (1987) Market-inalienability. Harv Law Rev 100(8):1849–1937
Sandel MJ (1982) Liberalism and the limits of justice. Cambridge University Press, Cambridge
Schechtman M (2018) The constitution of selves. Cornell University Press
Tadros V (2016) Wrongs and crimes. Oxford University Press
Taylor C (1995) The dialogical self. In: Goodman RF, Fisher WR (eds) Rethinking knowledge: Reflections across the disciplines. State University of New York Press, p 57–66
Tobia KP (2015) Personal identity and the Phineas Gage effect. Analysis 75(3):396–405
Wallace K (2019) The network self: relation, process, and personal identity. Routledge
Wardrope A (2015) Liberal individualism, relational autonomy, and the social dimension of respect. Int J Fem Approaches Bioeth 8(1):37–66

Wendt A (1994) Collective identity formation and the international state. Am Polit Sci Rev 88(2): 384–396

Westlund AC (2009) Rethinking relational autonomy. Hypatia 24(4):26–49

Williams RA (2008) Deception, mistake and vitiation of the victim's consent. Law Q Rev 124:132–159

Ysseldyk R (2017) Communicating religious identities. In: Oxford research encyclopedia of communication

Ysseldyk R, Matheson K, Anisman H (2010) Religiosity as identity: toward an understanding of religion from a social identity perspective. Personal Soc Psychol Rev 14(1):60–71

Ysseldyk R, McQuaid RJ, McInnis OA, Anisman H, Matheson K (2018) The ties that bind: Ingroup ties are linked with diminished inflammatory immune responses and fewer mental health symptoms through less rumination. PLoS One 13(4):e0195237

Chapter 10
Concluding Remarks

10.1 Contribution

The central contribution of this book has been a novel argument for reconceptualising personal identity in the sexual offences context. A foundational assumption has been that the concept of identity, and the question of identity persistence, is not merely of abstract, metaphysical interest. It has philosophical, social, and legal-political significance. Accordingly, the book has incorporated philosophical, social, and legal aspects of the notion of identity. This provided the foundation for a thesis that is analytically and theoretically grounded.

10.2 Summary

This book has argued that the law ought to prohibit qualitative identity impersonation, and that this could be achieved by reading s. 76(2)(b) (the impersonation provision) of the Sexual Offences Act 2003 more expansively. A novel equivalence thesis in three stages sought to show that one may impersonate not just other living persons, but also other dead persons, earlier selves, fictitious persons and, ultimately, different aspects of oneself. This thesis drew upon a dynamic, socio-relational understanding of identity, supplemented with a Substantial Difference Argument, to challenge the distinction drawn in law between identity, on the one hand, and traits and attributes on the other. By positing an intersubjective, relational self, we were able to articulate a broader range of identity deceptions—those centring on *what kind of person* D claims to be. In sum, while D-as-consent-seeker (at time t1) and D-as-sexual-penetrator (at time t2) may be numerically identical in a strict sense, they are legally non-identical on the broader understanding of identity. Therefore, where there is qualitative dissimilarity of the right kind, D-as-sexual-penetrator may be liable under the 2003 Act.

R. Farah, *Rereading Identity Deception in the UK Sexual Offences Act 2003*, SpringerBriefs in Law, https://doi.org/10.1007/978-3-031-44475-3_10

In making the case for broadening the scope of prohibited identity deceptions, the book takes numerical identity as the starting point. The 2003 Act assumes the concept of identity in the sense of reidentification. Thus, s. 76(2)(b) requires that V know D personally. To know someone personally is to recognise (having direct knowledge of) them as one and the same person at different points in time. The orthodox view is that reidentification is not satisfied by qualitative identity. Indeed, reidentification is compatible with a substantial amount of change.[1] This book has challenged that sharp division. In doing so, it reflects a growing body of literature placing pressure on the dichotomy between numerical and qualitative identity. It also aligns with theoretical and empirical contributions which highlight additional concepts, such as self-continuity, qualitative similarity, and the self-concept. Just as the reidentification question is expected to reflect our future concern, sexual offences law should adopt that conception (or conceptions) of identity which addresses what people most care about in exercising their sexual autonomy. The impersonation provision can accommodate a broader reading in line with what matters to people about personal identity in sexual matters.

10.3 Theoretical Framework

The book has set out a theoretical framework for understanding identity deception in sexual offences. This combines the insights of two prominent identity theorists: Kathleen Wallace and Charles Taylor. While Wallace's account helps to explain the dynamic, variable, and expansive nature of personal traits, Taylor fills the gap left by the neglect of moral and interpersonal aspects of selfhood. Together, I called this the *Network of Selves in Moral-Relational Space* lens. This framework anchored the discussion in Part III.

10.4 Methodological Approach

The methodological approach taken in this book has three main advantages. First, it draws on a wide range of literature, including philosophical, theoretical, and psychological-experimental, to ensure a comprehensive and well-grounded thesis. Furthermore, the approach combines metaphysical discussion with normative argument. This supports the book's normative implications, with a view to legal reform. Secondly, it takes a pluralistic approach to the question of identity, expressing a range of theoretical insights. This includes work that challenges the dichotomy between qualitative and numerical identity and recent studies on the emerging importance of moral and social traits. The third advantage is its argumentative

[1] Woike et al. (2020).

starting point: s. 76(2)(b) of the 2003 Act. This anchors the thesis in positive law and supports an argument from consistency. It is hoped that this approach lends credibility to the thesis overall, such that even legal theorists and practitioners with a different view of personal identity could endorse its conclusions.

10.5 Case Studies

To bring the central thesis of the book home, this section explores the possibility of a different outcome and/or reasoning in two important cases: *R v Jheeta*[2] *(with reference to R v B*[3]*)* and *R v Linekar.*[4] I have chosen these cases because I think they present the greatest challenge for an impersonation reading. Although I agree with the conviction for rape in *Jheeta*, I suggest different legal reasoning. Unencumbered by the narrow understanding of identity in the 2003 Act, and equipped with my analytical-theoretical framework, I bring the qualitative aspects of identity to the surface. The aim is to show that such cases can be brought within s. 76(2)(b)'s conclusive presumption, thereby avoiding reliance on s. 74. Similarly, with *Linekar*, I suggest that this can be explained as a deception as to identity case. For the sake of the discussion to follow, I shall assume that the arguments made in the preceding chapters go through.

10.5.1 R v Jheeta

The facts of *Jheeta* were as follows: D (the appellant) and V (the complainant) were in a sexual relationship. As the relationship cooled, V began to receive anonymous threatening text messages, which in fact D had been sending to her. V had confided in D and sought to alert the police. D then escalated the deception. Pretending to be a fictitious policeman, he continued to threaten V, as well as blackmailing her. Believing that she would receive a fine if she did not continue to have sex with D, V had sexual intercourse with him over several years. Alongside other offences, D was rightly convicted of rape based on the coercive pressure placed on V.

The court made clear that the conclusive presumption under s. 76(2)(a) will only rarely arise and does not apply to 'disingenuous blandishments of or common or garden lies.'[5] Such deception must go to the nature or purpose of the act, which is sexual intercourse. Otherwise, it is to be dealt with under s 74. Similarly, it was not an impersonation case under s. 76(2)(b). This was because V was not deceived that

[2] [2007] EWCA Crim 1699.

[3] [2013] EWCA Crim 823.

[4] [1995] QB 250, [1995] s All ER 230.

[5] *Jheeta* (n 2) [24] [27] (Lord Justice Judge).

she was having sex with her boyfriend. The court illustrated the limited role of s. 76 by reference to several cases, most notably *Linekar*. Because the deception in that case related to D's *intentions*, s. 76 had no application. Equally in this case, V was deceived merely about the situation she was in, which the courts treat as a peripheral matter. This left the matter to be decided under s. 74's general definition of consent, which found that she had not consented freely on at least some occasions.[6]

10.5.1.1 Alternative Reasoning

This case could have been framed as deception as to identity under s. 76(2)(b) if only a richer understanding of identity were available. Indeed, the case raises difficult questions around the narrow personal knowing condition of the subsection. Per the continuum outlined in Chap. 8, it concerned someone whom V knew *intimately* pretending to be someone she did not know *personally*. *R v B* has a similar same structure. In both cases, it was V's boyfriend engaging in *fictitious other impersonation* to both trick and pressurise V into sexual activity. While in *Jheeta*, V knew that she was having sex with her boyfriend, in *B*, V thought the sexual gratification was for someone else.[7] This suggests that *B* might be likely to succeed as an impersonation case, subject to a revised personal knowing condition. It seems incongruous, then, that *Jheeta* should fail.

The court's reasoning reveals a narrow focus on whether V was mistaken about whom she was having sex with. However, this lacks moral relevance when the requisite three elements were present: impersonation, taking advantage of personal knowing (properly defined), and causing V to consent. In both cases, V agreed to sex / sexual acts for the benefit of someone she thought was a stranger but who was actually her boyfriend. What moral justification is there for requiring that the impersonation be, in addition, operative, or 'live', at the time of sexual activity? It is understandable that the courts are reluctant to find s. 76 applicable because it 'removes D's last line of defence.'[8] It is important from a rule of law perspective to exercise caution with the conclusive presumptions. However, I think there are two objections to this judicial reluctance.

As a preliminary point, such reluctance is not entirely convincing given that D can avoid the application of s. 76 quite easily by adopting a personal commitment not to deceive V into consenting to sex. But secondly, it seems morally relevant in *Jheeta* that having committed impersonation, D then stepped back into his own identity to take advantage of his achievement. This is a 'change of normative

[6] Ibid. [29] (Lord Justice Judge).

[7] Assuming online interactions do not satisfy the known personally requirement and that knowing personally is not satisfied by knowing an immediate family member. As an indirect kind of personal knowing., it seems to sit in between knowing *of* someone and knowing someone personally.

[8] *B* (n 3) [20] (Lord Justice Hallett).

position[9] that one could argue makes him more blameworthy than the defendant in *B*. At least, it seems clear that he is not *less* blameworthy. As Gardner argues in defence of constructive liability relating to assault, by committing the original unlawful act, you change your normative position and are liable for any unintended consequences.[10] Equally, by committing impersonation, D crosses the threshold into deception as to identity. The criminal law attaches normative significance to a person's level of commitment to wrongdoing. This is reflected in the inchoate offences, as well as, though more controversially, in preparatory offences. Accordingly, sexual offences law could focus on the fact that V agreed to have sex to satisfy the demands of the impersonator. And it could prevent liability from hinging on whether he removed his 'mask' or left it on to perform the sexual act.

My theoretical framework lends further support to a different outcome. I think it illuminates four aspects relevant to impersonation: significant change to an intimate relationship (who D is conflicts with the nature of the relationship); change to one's orientation in moral-relational space; loss of an identity-defining community; and change to a hub.

I mentioned earlier that because V knew with whom she was having sex, this ruled out the impersonation provision. But in a qualitative sense, she had no idea with whom she was having sex. D was a man with whom she was (supposed to be) in a caring, intimate relationship. Such relationships are central to self-identity,[11] Yet, D was someone else entirely. The relevant fact about him was not that he was her boyfriend; it was that he was hostile to her interests, that he intended her harm. In this respect, he was *impersonating* a boyfriend. Similarly, in *Linekar*, the relevant fact about D was not that he was 'John' or 'Jack'; it was that he was (supposed to be) V's client. Instead, he was *impersonating* a client. In a relational sense, being neither a boyfriend nor a client, D is like a different person. Indeed, if we think of identity as narrative, Lindemann's theory of 'good holding' is relevant.[12] Had V known the truth, she would have 'let go' of D in his identities. She would have imagined new stories in relation to him. This is a proxy for identity change.[13]

Such change also implicates one's orientation in moral-relational space. It is surely normatively significant that the person V had sex with was her threatener-blackmailer. We can frame this in terms of moral deterioration, in line with the moral self effect discussed in Chap. 5. Romantic partners share communal relationships, whereas this turned out to be an exchange relationship.[14] We can also frame it by reference to D's orientation towards the good and to his intimate relations. These

---

[9] I borrow this notion from Gardner (1994).

[10] Ibid, p. 509.

[11] Herring (2019); Taylor (1992).

[12] Lindemann (2014).

[13] This might rely on assuming an autobiographical account of narrativity, but not necessarily. Even if D writes his own stories, he cannot do so in isolation from interaction with, and influence of, others.

[14] Clark and Mills (1979).

were starkly different to that which he presented to V. This deception reflects what *kind* of person D is. In keeping with this book's thesis, it reflects personal identity in a qualitative sense, which matters greatly. Indeed, having sex with an unsuspecting loved one to avoid personal harm threatened by another person is one thing; having sex with the person who is doing the harming is quite another.

10.5.2 R v Linekar

The facts of *Linekar* were as follows: V, a prostitute, had agreed to sexual intercourse with D for payment. D refused to pay afterwards and had never intended to pay. Having been convicted of rape, the Court of Appeal overturned this decision, finding that there had been no deception as to the nature or purpose of the act, nor to identity—this latter point confirmed in *Jheeta.*[15] V knew that it was a sexual act, that D's purpose was sexual gratification, and she knew who D was. She did not mistake D for another person. Whatever D's intention, this was not relevant to the question of consent.

10.5.2.1 Alternative Reasoning

V mistook D for a different *kind* of person, and this was the only kind of identity that mattered to her. As noted earlier, what mattered was that he was a 'client' who would pay her. This *mattering* recalls Taylor's rejection of the 'neutral' self.[16] Equally, the relevant aspect of V's identity was that she was a prostitute. Thus, she was not seeking casual sex with D. She sought to conclude a transaction exchanging sex for money. I will now flesh out this reasoning.

First, there is a neglected issue that is relevant to the question of identity. I suggest that the concept of recognition, conceived by Honneth and developed by Taylor,[17] was salient in this case. More precisely, there was a failure of mutual recognition between V and D. This stemmed from the fact that what was ostensibly a prostitute-client relationship was, in fact, not. We might characterise it as a 'prostitute-non client' relationship. Or instead as a 'non-prostitute-non-client' relationship. This latter characterisation reflects the fact that if D is, objectively, not a client, then V cannot be selling sex to him. And if she is not selling sex, she must just be *having* sex. Therefore, D's deception might be said to inflict identity non-recognition on V, which Kennedy conceptualises as a distinct wrong of rape.[18] Moreover, if sexual

[15] *Jheeta* (n 2) [27].

[16] Taylor (1992), p. 49.

[17] Honneth (1995); Taylor (1994).

[18] Kennedy (2021).

relations is a hub in Wallace's sense, then D's deception constitutes significant change to a hub as they are engaged not in transactional sex but casual sex.

Yet, some commentators argue that rape in these circumstances is not clearly harmful in the way it would be if V were not a prostitute.[19] On this view, because a prostitute seems to value her sexuality less highly (seemingly evidenced in her decision to sell sex), she cannot be harmed in the same way as others. I reject this. Whereas Murphy suggests that the prostitute might regard her sexuality as a commodity to be sold rather than 'a sacred and mysterious aspect of her self-identity,'[20] the better view is that when she sells sex, she subordinates her sexuality for the time being and simply does not bring this aspect of her self-identity into the interaction. In other words, she so values her sexuality that she has strategies to reflexively separate it from the sexual act. Moreover, Murphy's view ignores the constrained nature of choice.

With this in mind, we might think of prostitution not as the purchase or commodification of sex, or a body, but as the purchase of *subordination*. Indeed, that D wishes not merely to subordinate V but to inflict humiliation on her, reveals a great deal about what kind of person he is. I suggest that inflicting humiliation reflects change to a (sexual relations) 'hub' in Wallace's terms; we should consider it as *other* than sex. In the language of community and communities discussed in Chap. 6, there is deception as to community in that D has rejected the shared meanings of the community of sexual participants.[21] Similarly, in *B*,[22] where D inflicted sexual perversion and degradation upon V rather than the sexual-relational intimacy appropriate to the relationship. On Archer's terms,[23] D's identity is *constituted* by such a commitment. Per Hitlin,[24] D's values (or absence thereof) reveal the core of his identity. And drawing on Greenwood's account,[25] we might explain D's behaviour according to the norm internalisation traceable to his membership of a misogynistic group identity. Finally, insofar as D presented himself as a client, his identity was bounded by what Archer calls 'the unthinkable'.[26] That he was, in fact, a sexual-violator-masquerading-as-a-client shows that his identity was not bounded in the way V was led to believe. In this sense, he was a different kind of person.

Secondly, the *Network of Selves in Moral-Relational Space lens* offers a richer perspective for understanding the wrong of identity deception. More precisely, I think there are two possible ways this lens can support a different outcome in *Linekar*. The first is relatively straightforward; *major change to a hub* was one of several grounds outlined in Chap. 6 and developed from Wallace's work. Consider

---

[19] See Feinberg (1986); Murphy (1994).

[20] Murphy (1994), p. 216.

[21] I will say more about this shortly.

[22] *B* (n 3).

[23] Archer (2015).

[24] Hitlin (2003).

[25] Greenwood (1994).

[26] Archer (2015).

the difference between someone being a prostitute and not being a prostitute. Arguably, this tracks major change to a hub (e.g., class, intersectional, and/or sexual-relational). However, the locus of such change is V rather than D.[27] Thinking instead about D, we might say that the difference between someone who uses and does not use prostitutes tracks major change to a hub, but this does not seem obvious. Instead, I think this is likely better explained via two routes.

The first accords with the notion of social or moral traits, which I developed in Chap. 6 from Taylor's work. This route involves attending to the way in which D's deception represents a breach of community values. Plausibly, such values can tolerate deception. But D chose to exploit someone who was already structurally disadvantaged and situationally vulnerable, making her materially worse off. Such conduct is especially egregious—even more so because of the nature of V's sacrifice as a sex worker who must subordinate her sexuality to D and alienate this aspect of her self-identity. There may be a way of formulating this reading in legally certain terms, though I will not attempt to do so here. In sum, when we draw out the qualitative aspects of identity and ask in what ways they matter in the scenario, and to whom, we can reach a different outcome in *Linekar*.

The second relates to the notion of community and communities in the work of Taylor and Wallace. Building on Wallace's account of 'experiential parallelism',[28] we can posit a community of sexual actors sharing the common experience of sexual relations, and a sub-community of sex-workers and sex-customers within this larger community. Insofar as D's deception was incompatible with the shared meaning that defined their community of sexual transactors, there could be deception as to community. In deceiving V, D pretended that his defining community was other than it was. Per Taylor, our relation to a defining community is one dimension of our identity definition.

In sum, a richer understanding of identity in terms of its qualitative aspects can support different outcomes in key cases of sexual deception involving identity. The book has presented a diverse arsenal of theoretical and philosophical tools to support a different interpretation of identity. From moral and social traits, a person's guiding commitments (including what he or she is committed *not* to do), and core values, to identity-defining relationships, intimate relations, and the role of 'holding and letting go'—I think there is ample reason to rethink our approach to identity deception in sexual relations.

---

[27] Although identity non-recognition could be argued here. See Kennedy (2021) for an identity argument based on V's perspective.

[28] Wallace (2019), p. 118.

10.6 Future Directions

In terms of future directions, this book has the potential to stimulate further thinking about the insights to be gleaned from personal identity theory. The subject of impersonation would benefit from further scholarship, perhaps taking the moral question as an alternative starting point or considering identity instead as a characterisation question for the purpose of sexual offences law. Finally, I hope that this book, by clarifying the meaning of identity and developing a new approach to its application in law, might be of value to the social sciences in general.

Cases

R v B [2013] EWCA Crim 823
R v Devonald [2008] EWCA Crim 527
R v Jheeta [2007] 2 Cr App R 477
R v Linekar [1995] 2 CAR 49
CrimA 5734/10 Kashur v. State of Israel [2012], Takdin (Isr.), Nevo Legal Database

Legislation

Sexual Offences Act 2003, s. 76(2)(a), s. 76(2)(b)

References

Archer M (2015) The relational subject and the person: self, agent, and actor. In: Donati P, Archer M (eds) The relational subject. Cambridge University Press, pp 85–122
Clark MS, Mills J (1979) Interpersonal attraction in exchange and communal relationships. J Pers Soc Psychol 37(1):12
Feinberg J (1986) Harm to self: the moral limits of the criminal law, vol 3. Oxford University Press, Oxford
Gardner J (1994) Rationality and the rule of law in offences against the person. Camb Law J 53(3): 502–523
Greenwood JD (1994) A sense of identity: prolegomena to a social theory of personal identity. J Theory Soc Behav 24(1):25–46
Herring J (2019) Law and the relational self. Cambridge University Press
Hitlin S (2003) Values as the core of personal identity: drawing links between two theories of self. Soc Psychol Q 66:118–137
Honneth A (1995) The struggle for recognition—the moral grammar of social conflicts. Polity Press, Cambridge
Kennedy C (2021) Criminalising deceptive sex: sex, identity and recognition. Leg Stud 41(1): 91–110

Lindemann H (2014) Holding and letting go: the social practice of personal identities, Online edn. Oxford Academic. https://doi.org/10.1093/acprof:oso/9780199754922.001.0001
Murphy J (1994) Some ruminations on women, violence, and the criminal law. In: Coleman J, Buchanan A (eds) In harm's way: essays in honour of Joel Feinberg. Cambridge University Press
Taylor C (1992) Sources of the self: the making of the modern identity. Cambridge University Press
Taylor C (1994) The politics of recognition. In: Gutmann A (ed) Multiculturalism: examining the politics of recognition. Princeton University Press, Princeton
Wallace K (2019) The network self: relation, process, and personal identity. Routledge
Woike JK, Collard P, Hood B (2020) Putting your money where your self is: connecting dimensions of closeness and theories of personal identity. PLoS One 15(2):e0228271

MIX
Papier aus verantwortungsvollen Quellen
Paper from responsible sources
FSC® C105338

If you have any concerns about our products,
you can contact us on
ProductSafety@springernature.com

In case Publisher is established outside the EU,
the EU authorized representative is:
Springer Nature Customer Service Center GmbH
Europaplatz 3, 69115 Heidelberg, Germany

Printed by Libri Plureos GmbH
in Hamburg, Germany